LITERATURE FROM CRESCENT MOON PUBLISHING

The Ecstasies of John Cowper Powys
by A.P. Seabright

Postmodern Powys: New Essays on John Cowper Powys
by Joe Boulter

Thomas Hardy and John Cowper Powys: Wessex Revisited
by Jeremy Mark Robinson

Sexing Hardy: Thomas Hardy and Feminism
by Margaret Elvy

Thomas Hardy's Jude the Obscure: A Critical Study
by Margaret Elvy

Thomas Hardy's Tess of the d'Urbervilles: A Critical Study
by Margaret Elvy

Thomas Hardy: The Tragic Novels
by Tom Spenser

Stepping Forward: Essays, Lectures and Interviews
by Wolfgang Iser

Lawrence Durrell: Between Love and Death, Between East and West
by Jeremy Mark Robinson

Andrea Dworkin
by Jeremy Mark Robinson

German Romantic Poetry: Goethe, Novalis, Heine, Hölderlin, Schlegel, Schiller
by Carol Appleby

Rilke: Space, Essence and Angels in the Poetry of Rainer Maria Rilke
by B.D. Barnacle

Rimbaud: Arthur Rimbaud and the Magic of Poetry
by Jeremy Mark Robinson

Shakespeare: Love, Poetry and Magic in Shakespeare's Sonnets and Plays
by B.D. Barnacle

Cavafy: Anatomy of a Soul
by Matt Crispin

Feminism and Shakespeare
by B.D. Barnacle

The Poetry of Landscape in Thomas Hardy
by Jeremy Mark Robinson

D.H. Lawrence: Infinite Sensual Violence
by M.K. Pace

D.H. Lawrence: Symbolic Landscapes
by Jane Foster

The Passion of D.H. Lawrence
by Jeremy Mark Robinson

Samuel Beckett Goes Into the Silence
by Jeremy Mark Robinson

In the Dim Void: Samuel Beckett's Late Trilogy: Company, Ill Seen, Ill Said and Worstward Ho
by Gregory Johns

Andre Gide: Fiction and Fervour in the Novels
by Jeremy Mark Robinson

Julia Kristeva: Art, Love, Melancholy, Philosophy, Semiotics
by Kelly Ives

Luce Irigaray: Lips, Kissing, and the Politics of Sexual Difference
by Kelly Ives

Hélène Cixous I Love You: The Jouissance of Writing
by Kelly Ives

Emily Dickinson: *Selected Poems*
selected and introduced by Miriam Chalk

Petrarch, Dante and the Troubadours: The Religion of Love and Poetry
by Cassidy Hughes

Dante: *Selections From the Vita Nuova*
translated by Thomas Okey

Friedrich Hölderlin: *Selected Poems*
translated by Michael Hamburger

Rainer Maria Rilke: *Selected Poems*
translated by Michael Hamburger

Wolfgang Iser's books include *The Implied Reader* (1974), *The Act of Reading* (1978), *Prospecting* (1989) and *The Fictive and the Imaginary* (1993). He has written books on Laurence Sterne (1988) and Walter Pater (1987). He is Professor of English and Comparative Literature at the University of Constance in Germany.

STEPPING FORWARD

STEPPING FORWARD

Essays, Lectures and Interviews

Wolfgang Iser

CRESCENT MOON

Crescent Moon Publishing
P.O. Box 393
Maidstone
Kent
ME14 5XU, U.K.

First published 2000. Second edition 2008.
© Wolfgang Iser, 2000, 2008.

Printed and bound in Great Britain
Set in Book Antiqua 9 on 14pt.

The right of Wolfgang Iser to be identified as the author of this book has been asserted generally in accordance with sections 77 and 78 of the Copyright, Designs and Patents Act 1988

All rights reserved. No part of this book may be reprinted or reproduced, stored in a retrieval system, or transmitted, in any form or by any means, electronic, mechanical, photocopying, recording or otherwise, without permission from the publisher.

British Library Cataloguing in Publication data

Stepping Forward: essays, lectures and interviews
1. Literature – History and criticism
2. Books and reading
I. Title

ISBN 1-86171-168-9
ISBN-13 1861711687

CONTENTS

The Significance of Fictionalizing   15
The Centre for British Studies
and Its Contribution to a Study of Culture   33
Eureka: *The* Interpretation of *Tom Jones*   47
Interview (1984)   57
An Interview with Wolfgang Iser   67

THE SIGNIFICANCE OF FICTIONALIZING

If a literary text does something to its readers, it also simultaneously tells us something about them. Thus literature turns into a divining rod, locating our dispositions, desires, inclinations, and eventually our overall makeup. The question arises as to why we may need this particular medium, especially in view of the fact that literature as a medium is put on a par with other media, and the ever-increasing role that these play in our civilization shows the degree to which literature has lost its significance as the epitome of culture. The more comprehensively a medium fulfils its sociocultural function, the more it is taken for granted, as literature once used to be. It did indeed fulfil several such functions, ranging from entertainment through information and documentation to pastime, but these have now been distributed among many independent institutions that not only compete fiercely with literature but also deprive it of its formerly all-encompassing function. Does literature still have anything to offer that the competing media are unable to provide?

WOLFGANG ISER   STEPPING FORWARD

I shall try to address this question by focusing on the fictionality of literature, first by detailing how to conceive of ficitonalizing, and second by suggesting why we as human beings may need this form of make-believe.

Most people associate the term fiction with the story-telling branch of literature, but in its other guise it is also what Dr Johnson called 'a falsehood; a lye' (1755). The equivocalness of the word is very revealing, for each meaning sheds light on the other. Both meanings entail similar processes, which we might term 'overstepping' what is: the lie oversteps the truth, and the literary work oversteps the real world which it incorporates. It is therefore not surprising that literary fictions were so often branded as lies, since they talk of what does not exist, even though they present its non-reality as if it did exist.

Plato's complaint that poets lie met its first strong opposition in the Renaissance, when Sir Philip Sidney rejoined that 'the Poet... nothing affirmeth, and therefore never lieth,'[1] since he does not talk of what is, but of what ought to be, and this form of overstepping is quite different from lying. Fiction and fictionalizing entail a duality, the liar must conceal the truth, but the truth is potentially present in the mask disguising it. In literary fictions, existing worlds are overstepped, and although they are individually still recognizable, they are set in a context that defamiliarizes them. Thus both lie and literature contain two worlds: the lie incorporates the truth and the purpose for which it must be concealed; literary fictions incorporate an identifiable reality that is subjected to an unforeseeable refashioning. And when we describe fictionalizing as an act of overstepping, we must bear in mind that the reality overstepped is not left behind: it remains present, thereby imbuing fiction with a duality that may be exploited for different purposes. In what is to follow, we shall focus on fictionalizing as a means of actualizing the possible in order to address the question why human beings, in spite of their awareness that literature is make-believe, seem to stand in need of fictions.

Even if nowadays literary fictions are no longer charged with lying, they are still stigmatized as being unreal, regardless of the vital role fictions play in our everyday lives. In his book *Ways of Worldmaking,*[2] Nelson Goodman shows that we do not live in one reality but in many, and each of these realities is the result of a processing which can never be traced back to 'something stolid underneath.'[3] There is no single underlying world, but instead we create new worlds out of old ones in a process which Goodman describes as 'fact from fiction.'[4] Fictions, then, are not the unreal side of reality, let alone the opposite of reality, which our 'tacit knowledge' still takes them to be; they are, rather, conditions that enable the production of worlds whose reality, in turn, is not to be doubted.

Such ideas were first articulated by Sir Francis Bacon, who argues that fictions 'give some shadow of satisfaction to the mind… in those points wherein the nature of things doth deny it."[5] This is not quite the same as Goodman's ways of worldmaking, but it shows how we can gain access to the inaccessible by inventing possibilities. It is a view that has survived down the ages, and four hundred years later Marshall McLuhan described the 'art of fiction' as an extension of man.[6]

This may be one of the reasons why we cannot talk of fiction as such, for it can only be described by way of its functions, that is, the manifestations of its use and the products resulting from it. This is evident even to cursory observation: in epistemology we find fictions as pre-suppositions; in science they are hypotheses; fictions provide the foundations for world-pictures; and the assumptions that guide our actions are fictions as well. In each of these cases, fiction has a different task to perform: with epistemological positing, it is a premise; with the hypothesis, it is a test; with world-pictures, it is a dogma whose fictional nature must remain concealed if the foundation is not to be impaired; and with our actions, it is anticipation. Since fictions have such manifold applications, we might well ask what they appear to be like, and what they reveal in literature.

Undoubtedly, the literary text is permeated by a vast range of identifiable items selected from social and other extratextual realities. The mere importation of such realities into the text – even though they are not being represented in the text for their own sake – does not *ipso facto* make them fictive. Instead, the text's apparent reproduction of items from the world outside serves to highlight purposes, intentions, and aims that are decidedly not part of the realities reproduced. Hence they appear in the text as a product of a fictionalizing act, which converts the realities concerned into a sign for something other than themselves.

As the creation of an author, the literary text evidences a particular attitude through which the author directs himself or herself to the world. Therefore each text makes inroads into extratextual fields of reference and, by disrupting them, creates an eventful disorder. In consequence, both structure and semantics of these fields are subject to certain deformations. Each one is reshuffled in the text and takes on a new form, a form that nevertheless includes, and indeed depends on, the very function this field has within the structure of the given world. This function now becomes virtual and provides the background against which the operation of restructuring may stand out in relief, featuring the intention underlying the apparent deformation. Furthermore, the ensuing tension indicates that the referential world which has been overstepped is still present in the text. Every literary text inevitably contains a selection from a variety of social, historical, cultural and literary systems that exist as referential fields outside the text.

A complement to the act of selection is the act of combination, which is also an act of fictionalizing, marked by the same basic mode of operation: the crossing of boundaries. Here the boundaries that are crossed are intratextual, ranging from lexical meanings to the constellation of characters. On the lexical level this is to be seen, for instance, with neologisms such as Joyce's coining of the term *benefiction*, which combines the words benefaction, benediction, and fiction. The lexical meaning of a particular word is faded out and a new meaning faded in, without the loss of the original meaning. This establishes a figure-and-ground relationship, allowing both the separation of the individual elements and a continuous switching of the perspective between them. In accordance with whichever reference forms the foreground or background, the semantic weighting will be shifted.

Another level of relating is to be seen in the organization of specific semantic demarcations within the text. These give rise to intratextual fields of reference, which provide an occasion for the hero of a novel, for instance, to step over internally marked boundaries. Such boundary-crossing is a subject-creating event.[7] It is 'revolutionary' insofar as it infringes on an intratextual organization.

The various clusters, whether they be words with out-stripped meanings or semantic demarcations transgressed by the characters in a narrative, are inseparably linked; they inscribe themselves into one another, every word becomes dialogic, and every intratextual semantic field is doubled by another. Through this double-voiced discourse every utterance carries something else in its wake, and thus the acts of combination unfold a play space between them in which the present is always doubled by the absent, frequently redistributing the weight by making the present totally subservient to the absent: what is said ceases to mean itself, so that what is not said can thus gain presence. There is no third dimension in the text that would allow to relate precisely what is related to what; instead, the double meaning of words as well as the elements selected from outside the text and now yoked together in an unfamiliar way are related through the different influences they have upon one another.

Fictions also play vital roles in the activities of cognition and behaviour, as in the founding of institutions, societies, and world-pictures. Unlike such non-literary fictions, the literary text reveals its own fictionality. Because of this, its function must be radically different from that of related activities that mask their fictional nature. The masking, of course, need not necessarily occur with the intention to deceive; it occurs because the fiction is meant to provide an explanation, or even a foundation, and would not do so if its fictive nature were to be exposed. The concealment of fictionality endows an explanation with an appearance of reality, which is vital, because fiction – as explanation – functions as the constitutive basis of this reality.

When a fiction signals its own fictionality – for which of course literary genres are the most obvious and durable signs – it necessitates an attitude different from that adopted toward fictions hiding their fictionality. The incorporated 'real' world is, so to speak, put in brackets, simultaneously indicating that it is to be viewed as if it were a world, a world, however, that has no empirical existence, and thus is only to be taken as if it were a given world. In the self-disclosure of its fictionality, an important feature of the fictional text comes to the fore: it places the world organized in the text under the sign of the 'as if'. Thus readers are signalled that they must bracketoff their natural attitudes toward what they are reading. But this does not mean forgetting or transcending those natural attitudes, which cannot be abandoned. Instead, they figure as a virtualized background, which as a latent instance of comparison, or at least as a testing ground, is essential if the textual world is to be digested. Thus the bracketing-off process splits the reader's attitude into one that is simultaneously natural and artificial. The natural attitude loses its validity, so that the new one may develop, but the new one would not achieve stability if it could not be played off against the old one.

Thus the purpose of the self-disclosing fiction comes to light. If the world represented in the literary text is not meant to denote a given world, and hence is turned into an analogue for figuring something, it serves two different purposes at once. The reaction provoked by the represented world could be directed toward conceiving what the textual world is meant to 'figure forth.' The analogue, however, could simultaneously direct the reaction to the empirical world from which the textual world was drawn, allowing this very world to be perceived from a vantage point that has never been part of it. In this case the reverse side of things will come into view. The duality of the analogue will never exclude either of the two possibilities; in fact, they appear to interpenetrate, making conceivable what would otherwise remain hidden.

All the acts of fictionalizing that can be distinguished within the fictional text are acts of boundary-crossing. Selection transgresses the limits of extratextual systems as well as the boundaries of the text itself by pointing to the referential fields that link the text to what is beyond the page. Combination transgresses the semantic demarcations established by the text, ranging from the derestriction of lexical meanings to the hero's infringement on strictly enforced borderlines. Finally, the 'as if' construction discloses the fictionality of fiction, thus transgressing the represented world set up by the acts of selection and combination, thereby indicating that it is to be used for an unverbalized, though overarching, purpose. The self-disclosure has a twofold significance. First, it shows that fiction can be known as fiction. Second, it shows that the re-presented world is only to be conceived as if it were a world in order that it should be taken to figure something other than itself.

Ultimately, the text brings about one more boundary-crossing that occurs within the reader's experience: it stimulates attitudes toward an unreal world, the unfolding of which leads to the temporary displacement of the reader's own reality. As the acts of fictionalizing are geared to one another and have a clearly punctuated sequence, their different types of boundary-crossing ensure assimilation of a transformed world that issues from them. The acts of fictionalizing can be clearly distinguished by the different gestalt each of them brings about: selection results in revealing the intentionality of the author; combination results in bringing about unfamiliar relationships of the items selected within the text; and self-disclosure results in bracketing the world represented, thereby converting it into a sign for something else, and simultaneously suspending the reader's natural attitude. All these cases are 'facts from fiction.'

Furthermore, the various acts of fictionalizing carry with them whatever has been outstripped, and the resultant doubleness might therefore be defined as the simultaneity of the mutually exclusive. All the fictionalizing acts discussed are marked by this doubleness. Selection opens up an area between fields of reference and their distortion in the text; combination opens up another between interacting textual segments; and the 'as if' opens up another between an empirical world and its transposition into an analogue for what remains unsaid though meant by the text. Thus the formula of fictionality as the simultaneity of the mutually exclusive allows for describing the structure of the fictional component of literature. It gives rise to a dynamic oscillation resulting in a constant interpenetration of things which are set off from one another without ever losing their difference. The tension ensuing from the attempt to resolve this ineradicable difference creates an æsthetic potential which, as a source of meaning, can never be substituted by anything else. This does not imply that the fictional component of literature is the actual work of art. What it does imply, however, is that the fictional component makes the work of art possible.

Now we have to take a look at what this doubling structure may imply, and, better still, what it might indicate. As a lead for addressing this issue, we might consider a passage in the novel *The Unbearable Lightness of Being* by the Czech writer Milan Kundera, who caused a stir with this particular piece of literature before European Communism collapsed.

> Staring impotently across the courtyard, at a loss for what to do; hearing the pertinacious rumbling of one's own stomach during a moment of love; betraying, yet lacking the will to abandon the glamorous path of betrayal; raising one's fist with the crowds in the Grand March; displaying one's wit before hidden microphones – I have known all these situations, I have experienced them myself, yet none of them has given rise to the person my curriculum vitæ and I represent. The characters in my novels are my unrealized possibilities. That is why I am equally fond of them all and equally horrified by them. Each one has crossed a border that I myself have circumvented. It is that crossed border (the border beyond which my own 'I' ends) which attracts me most. For beyond that border begins the secret the novel asks about. The novel is not the author's confession; it is an investigation of human life in the trap the world has become.'[8]

The possibilities Kundera speaks of lie beyond what is, even though they could not exist without what there is. This duality is brought into focus through writing, which is motivated by the desire to overstep the reality surrounding the novelist. Therefore he does not write about what there is, and this overstepping is related to a dimension that retains its equivocalness, for it depends on what is, yet cannot be derived from what there is.

On the one hand the writer's reality fades into a range of its own possibilities, and on the other these possibilities overstep what is and thus invalidate it. But this penumbra of possibilities could not have come into being if the world, to which it forms the horizon, had been left behind. Instead, they begin to uncover what hitherto had remained concealed in the very world now refracted in the mirror of possibilities, thus exposing it as a trap.

In the novel, then, the real and the possible coexist, for it is only the author's selection from and textual representation of the real world that can create a matrix for the possible to emerge, whose ephemeral character would remain shapeless if it were not the transformation of something already existing. But it would also remain meaningless if it did not serve to bring out the hidden areas of given realities. Having both the real and the possible and yet, at the same time, maintaining the difference between them – this is a process denied us in real life; it can only be staged in the form of the 'as if'. Otherwise, whoever is caught up in reality, cannot experience possibility, and vice versa. In what sense, though, is our world a 'trap,' and what compels us to overstep the boundaries? All fictionalizing authors do this, and so, too, do readers of literature who go on reading despite their awareness of the fictionality of the text. The fact that we seem to need this 'ecstatic' state of being beside, outside, and beyond ourselves, caught up in and yet detached from our own reality, derives from our inability to be present to ourselves. The ground out of which we are remains unavailable to us. Samuel Beckett's Malone says: 'Live or invent'[9] for as we do not know what it is to live, we must invent what eludes penetration. There is a similar dictum, equally pithy, by Helmuth Plessner, who corroborates Beckett from a rather different angle, that of social anthropology: 'I am, but I do not have myself'.[10] 'Have' means knowing what it is to be, which would require a transcendental stance in order to grasp the self-evident certainty of our existence with all its implications, significance and, indeed, meaning. If we wish to have what remains impenetrable, we are driven beyond ourselves; and as we can never be both ourselves and the transcendental stance to and of ourselves necessary to predicate what it means to be, we resort to fictionalizing. Beckett gave voice to what Plessner had posed as a problem: that self-fashioning is the answer to our inaccessibility to ourselves. Fictionalizing begins where knowledge leaves off, and this dividing line turns out to be the fountainhead of fiction by means of which we extend ourselves beyond ourselves.

The anthropological significance of fictionalizing becomes unmistakable in relation to the many unknowable realities permeating human life. Beginning and end are perhaps the most all-pervading realities of this kind. This means no less than that the cardinal points of our existence defy cognitive or even experiential penetration. The Greek physician Alkmaeon is believed to have earned Aristotle's approval when saying that human beings must die because they are not in the position to link up beginning and end.[11] If death is indeed the result of this impossibility, it is scarcely surprising that it should give rise to ideas that might lead to its abolition. These ideas would entail concocting possibilities in order to do away with what resists penetration, thus linking up ineluctable beginnings and endings and thereby creating a framework within which we might learn what it means to be caught up in life. The unending proliferation of such possibilities points to the fact that there are no means of authentication for the links provided. Instead, the fashioning of the unknowable will be determined to a large extent by historically prevailing needs. If fictionalizing transgresses those boundaries beyond which unrecognizable realities exist, then the very possibilities concocted for the repair of this deficiency, caught between our unknowable beginning and ending, become indicative of what is withheld, inaccessible, and unavailable. In this respect, fictionalizing turns out to be a measuring rod for gauging the historically conditioned changeability of deeply entrenched human desires.

If the borderlines of knowledge give rise to fictionalizing activity, we might perceive an economy principle at work: namely, what can be known need not to be staged again, and so fictionality always subsidizes the unknowable. This becomes strikingly obvious when human beings, in contra-distinction to the inaccessibility to beginnings and endings, are in full possession of what is or of what they are in. This applies to all evidential experiences of life, which, characterized by instantaneous certainty, embody the exact opposite of inaccessibility. Evidential experiences are in the nature of an epiphany.

Love is probably the most intense of these experiences, and it is also the central topic of staging in literature. It is far from being excluded from experience, but it is excluded from knowledge, because there is no knowledge of what evidential experience actually is, or because evidence seems to make all knowledge redundant. Evidential experiences evince indubitability, which obviously tempts us to start asking questions. Is this simply because we would like knowledge of what is guaranteed by other certainties? Jerome Bruner provided an answer to this question, when remarking in a different context: 'For the object of understanding human events is to sense the alternativeness of human possibility. And so there will be no end to interpretation.'[12] If so, then the staging of evidential experiences in literature is concerned with laying out alternatives for instantaneous certainty. Such a display, however, would seem to be without limits, since with evidential experiences one cannot separate the matter experienced from the appearance. This makes the alternatives endlessly proliferating, as is proved by the limitless possibilities of staged love in literature. Evidential experience is almost like an assault; it happens to us, and we are inside it. But the experience awakens in us a desire to look at what has happened to us, and this is when the evidence explodes into alternatives. These alternatives cannot make themselves independent; they remain linked to the evidential experience to which we want to gain access.

But this means that instantaneous certainties trigger the need for staging in exactly the same way as the cardinal mysteries. Now, however, we can see the decentred position of the human being, i.e. to be and not to have oneself, in a somewhat different light. Not being present to oneself is now only one of the spurs to staging, and in the visualization of certainty it springs from the opposite impulse of wishing to face oneself. However, if certainty cannot be understood as compensation for unavailabilities, this asymmetry reflects a craving for alternatives even to those experiences which provide immediate certainty.

This is the point at which literary fictions diverge from the fictions of our ordinary world. The latter are assumptions, hypotheses, presuppositions and, more often than not, the basis of world views, and may be said to complement reality. Frank Kermode calls them 'concord fictions'[13] because they close off something which by its very nature is open. Fictionalizing in literature, however, appears to have a different aim. To transgress otherwise inaccessible realities (beginning, end, and evidential experiences) can only come to fruition by staging what is withheld. This enactment is propelled by the drive to reach beyond oneself, yet not in order to transcend oneself, but to become available to oneself. If such a move arises out of a need for compensation, then this very need remains basically unfulfilled in literary fictions. For the latter are always accompanied by convention-governed signs that signalize the 'as if'-nature of all the possibilities they adumbrate. Consequently, such a staged compensation for what is missing in reality never conceals the fact that in the final analysis it is nothing but make-believe, and so ultimately all the possibilities opened up must be lacking in authenticity. What is remarkable, though, is the fact that our awareness of this inauthenticity does not stop us from continuing to fictionalize.

Why is that so, and why are we still fascinated by fictionality, whose self-disclosure reveals any hoped-for compensation as pure semblance? What accounts for the potency of semblance is the following:

(1) None of the possibilities concocted can be representative, for each one is nothing but a kaleidoscopic refraction of what it mirrors and is therefore potentially infinitely variable. Thus semblance allows for a limitless fashioning of those realities that are sealed off from cognitive penetration.

(2) The possibilities concocted never hide or bridge the rift between themselves and the unfathomable realities. Thus semblance invalidates all forms of reconciliation.

(3) Finally, the rift can be acted out in an infinite number of ways. Thus semblance lifts all restrictions on the modes according to which that play space may be utilized.

The semblance, however, gives vivid presence to intangible states of affairs so that they may penetrate into the conscious mind as if they were an object of perception. What can never become present, and what eludes cognition and knowledge and is beyond experience, can enter consciousness only through feigned representation, for consciousness has no barrier – as Freud has remarked – against the perceptible and no defence against the imaginable. Consequently, ideas can be brought forth in consciousness from an as yet unknown state of affairs, indicating that the presence of the latter does not depend on any preceding experience. – By the way, something similar may be said of the dream. Here, too, the dream thoughts are staged as they push something through into consciousness that is not identical to themselves.

Let us sum up by asking what the fictionalizing of literature reveals of the human makeup. If literature permits limitless patterning of human nature, we may infer that what we call human nature is rather a featureless plasticity that lends itself to a continual culture-bound repatterning. It furthermore indicates the inveterate urge of human beings to become present to themselves; this urge, however, will never issue into a definitive shape, because self-grasping arises out of overstepping limitations. Literature fans out human plasticity into a panoply of shapes, each of which is an enactment of self-confrontation. As a medium, it can only show all determinacy to be illusory. It even incorporates into itself the inauthenticity of all the human patterning it features, since this is the only way it can give presence to the protean character of what it is mediating. Perhaps this is the truth through which literature counters the awareness that it is an illusion, thereby resisting dismissal as mere deception.

Moreover, literature reveals that we are the possibilities of ourselves. But since we are the originators of these possibilities, we cannot actually be them – we are left dangling in-between what we have produced. To unfold ourselves as possibilities of ourselves and – instead of consuming them to meet the pragmatic demands of everyday life – displaying them for what they are in a medium created for such an exposure, literary fictions reveal a deeply entrenched disposition of the human makeup. What might this be? The following answers as to the necessity of fictionalizing suggest themselves: we can only be present to ourselves in the mirror of our own possibilities; or, as a monad in the Leibnitzian sense, we are determined by bearing all imaginable possibilities within ourselves; or we can only cope with the open-endedness of the world by means of the possibilities we derive from ourselves and project onto the world; or we are the meeting point of the manifold roles we are able to assume, in order to grasp what we make ourselves into. As none of the roles into which we can transform ourselves is representative of what is possible, humankind is driven to invent itself ever anew. If fictionalizing provides humankind with unlimited possibilities of self-extension, it also exposes the inherent deficiency of human beings – our fundamental inaccessibility to ourselves; owing to this gap within ourselves, we are bound to become creative.

But in the final analysis fictionalizing may not be equated with any of these alternative manifestations. Instead, it spotlights that the in-between state arising as an offshoot of boundary-crossing contains boundless options for human self-fashioning. Fictionalizing, then, may be considered as opening a play space between all the alternatives enumerated, thus setting off free play which militates against all determinations as untenable restrictions. In this sense, fictionalizing offers an answer to the problem which the Greek physician, Alkmaeon, regarded as insoluble: linking beginning and end together in order to create one last possibility through which the end, even if it cannot be overstepped, may at least be illusively postponed. Henry James once said: 'The success of a work of art… may be measured by the degree to which it produces a certain illusion; that illusion makes it appear to us for the time that we have lived another life – that we have had a miraculous enlargement of our experience.'[14]

A lecture for the Learned Societies' Luncheon, given at Irvine on February 24, 1997.

NOTES

1. Sir Philip Sidney, *The Defense of Poesie, The Prose Works*, III, ed. Albert Feuillerat, Cambridge University Press, p. 29.
2. Nelson Goodman, *Ways of Worldmaking*, Hassocks, 1978
3. Ibid., p. 6 and 9.
4. Ibid., pp. 102-107.
5. Francis Bacon, *The Advancement of Learning and new Atlantis*, ed. Thomas Case, London, 1974, p. 96.
6. See Marshall McLuhan, *Understanding Media: The Extensions of Man*, New York, 1964, pp. 42, 66, 107, 235 and 242.
7. See Jurij M. Lotman, *The Structure of the Artistic Text* (Michigan Slavic Contributions, 7), trans. Ronald Vroom, Ann Arbor, 1977, p. 234.
8. Milan Kundera, *The Unbearable Lightness of Being*, trans. Michael Henry Heim, New York, 1987, p. 221.
9. Samuel Beckett, *Malone Dies*, New York, 1956, p. 18.
10. Helmuth Plessner, "Die anthropologische Dimension der Geschichtlichkeit", in *Sozialer Wandel. Zivilisation und Fortschritt als Kategorien der soziologischen Theorie*, ed. Hans Peter Dreitzel, Neuwied, 1972, p. 160.
11. Aristotle, *Problemata, Works*, VIII, ed. E.S. Forster, Oxford, 1927, p. 916a.
12. Jerome Bruner, *Actual Minds, Possible Worlds*, Cambridge, Mass., 1986, p. 53.
13. Frank Kermode, *The Sense of an Ending: Studies in the Theory of Fiction*, New York, 1967, pp. 62-64.
14. Henry James, *Theory of Fiction*, ed. James E. Miller, Lincoln, Nebraska, 1972, p. 93.

THE CENTRE FOR BRITISH STUDIES AND ITS CONTRIBUTION TO A STUDY OF CULTURE

Lecture Given at the Opening of the Centre for British Studies

Humboldt University, Berlin

June 15, 1995

The Centre for British Studies has been established for several reasons. Politically it is a "token of the bond with Great Britain",[1] to which the City Council of Berlin wishes to give concrete expression. Intellectually, it is a response to the present situation of the humanities, which in almost all Western industrial nations are exposed to radical change. Experimentally, it is an institution designed to meet the challenges that multidisciplinary orientations pose for the humanities. What underlies these different motives is highlighted in the motion passed by the Berlin Senate: The Centre 'is meant to enhance mutual understanding of cultural, historical, economic, social and legal developments,' in order to 'eventually [...] contribute, through interdisciplinary research and teaching, to training and enabling new generations of students to think in both cultures.'[2]

In focusing on what the Centre is meant to achieve, we should look briefly at the rise of the humanities in Germany – not least as they are currently plagued by a crisis similar to the one that struck the study of rhetoric in the liberal arts schools at the end of the eighteenth century. Traditionally, rhetoric is one of the seven liberal arts that promised to teach the art of persuasion. As early as the sixteenth century, however, that promise turned out to be rather hard to implement,[3] and there was growing controversy as to how rhetoric was to be conceived in order to achieve its original objective. All the arguments, however, were mere compensations for the growing insight that the art of persuasion, in the final analysis, cannot be taught. The more this suspicion gained ground, the more inevitable was the demise of the study of rhetoric in the liberal arts schools.

At the threshold of the nineteenth century, a major response to this decline was the growing interest of the romantics in the native heritage of the national community and its vernacular tradition, out of which gradually arose the national philologies that still form the institutional structure of the humanities.[4] Philology, born as it was out of the spirit of the nation state, was for a long time taken for granted, since the nation was to find and to secure its *raison d'être* in the study of its own literature, history, and philosophy. The idea of the nation-state legitimized the humanities as much as the latter seemed to render an ideal expression of the former.

This idea found support in the firm belief that such a branch of knowledge provided education [*Bildung*], and the more secularization progressed through the age of Enlightenment, the more education emerged as an indispensable instrument of self-fashioning. Thus the development of the humanities in Germany must be seen as coexisting 'with the rise of an emphatic notion of personality formation [*Persönlich-keitsbildung*]. Herder, Goethe, Wilhelm von Humboldt and others advocated such a concept at the turn of the eighteenth to the nineteenth century, and Fichte, Schelling, Schleiermacher, and Hegel continued to shape and develop it. This concept of personality formation rests on the idea that education works as a force integral to a nation-state which is aimed at establishing an institution not only of the law',[5] but also of general human education [*allgemeine Menschenbildung*]. Hence the subsequent distinction between general education [*Bildung*] and vocational training [*Berufsaus-bildung*], which Humboldt formulated as follows: 'Whatever is required either by the demands of life or by one of its particular vocations [*Gewerbe*] must be isolated and can be acquired only after a general education has been completed. Whoever blends both will contaminate education [*Bildung*], the outcome of which are neither educated human beings nor fully-fledged citizens of their respective social class'.[6]

Even if the nation-state on which the humanities were based and out of which they have arisen need not necessarily be understood as the 'birth trauma of the humanities',[7] this basis has long since started to crumble. In fact, the idea of education itself has become outdated, not least as the purity that Humboldt emphasized did not lead to the personality formation that he had hoped for. How else could the barbarism of our own century have happened – a century in which education in its original sense has become fossilized?[8] In the meantime, the humanities have been caught up in an unceasing exercise of self-reflection – probably less in order to recover their traditionally unquestioned *raison d'être* than to ascertain their own function within the processes of modernization. Thus the humanities were sometimes considered as damage control for the offshoots of modernization,[9] and sometimes as its driving force.[10] Moreover, while the natural sciences gained in importance, the humanities seemed to turn into sanctuaries for the study of the past. In C.P. Snow's words, the humanities may have been valid as one of 'the two cultures',[11] but their validity was on shaky ground.

Through a historical coincidence, the German term *Geisteswissenschaften* ('humanities') happens, despite the burdensome legacy of German idealism, to be a loan translation from the English. When John Stuart Mill's *System of Logic* appeared in German in 1849, the term 'moral science,' which he used throughout, was rendered as *Geisteswissenschaft*. By 'moral science,' Mill meant 'both the norm-oriented "practical" disciplines of morality, politics, and æsthetics, and the descriptively and nomologially-oriented disciplines of psychology, ethology, and sociology [...] It is this very distinction that the term '*Geisteswissenschaften* blurs.'[12]

It is important to remind ourselves of this translation, as the term 'moral science' encompasses almost all the components pertinent to the study of culture that has always been blocked by the notion of spirit [*Geist*] prevalent in the humanities in Germany. The notion of spirit continued to be treated as a be-all and end-all, thus maintaining a tradition of academic institutions that had already run dry. It was towards the end of the eighteenth century that doubts were raised as to what the age of Enlightenment still considered the constancy of human nature; this was particularly the case in Anglo-Saxon countries, where a more sophisticated empiricism regarded the assumed constants of human nature at best as fictions that may have served a purpose in the past, but now had to be discarded because human nature could no longer be reduced to any essentials.

As a result, humans could no longer be described independently of time, location, and circumstances. Their environment became a vital concern, not least because they had created it as their own world through which – now that they were conceived of as unfathomable – they had manifested themselves. Clifford Geertz, the American ethnologist quite rightly claims that abandoning the idea of a constant human nature has led to the rise of a concept of culture – a man-made, artificial 'habitat' – as 'human nature does not exist and men are purely and simply what their culture makes them'.[13] The idea of culture as contextual to humankind began to attract attention at the historic moment when humans could no longer be conceptualized other than in terms of their responses to the challenges of their environment.[14] Thus the humanities were bound to turn into a study of culture – not so much in order to legitimize themselves again, but rather to shed light on a world in which the network of human activities was the be-all and end-all.

A study of culture does not exist as an academic discipline. The term 'cultural studies' that is currently in vogue reflects first and foremost a spontaneous dissatisfaction with the traditional humanities, and may thus be characterized by its lack of discipline. The study of culture, however, is an interdisciplinary enterprise, and as such its success will depend on a form of institutionalization. For interdisciplinarity is more than just a willingness to engage in dialogue; it takes over the position formerly occupied by spirit, human nature, and other allegedly universal be-all and end-alls. The term 'interdisciplinarity' designates nothing short of an antidote to such universals, thus allowing for two related considerations. First, interdisciplinary subject matters will not come into existence prior to collaboration between disciplines. Since there are no existing frames of reference for investigating interdisciplinary subject matters, all approaches have to evolve out of the constitution of these subject matters themselves. Second, for such joint efforts to succeed, different disciplines have to be tied together institutionally, thus ensuring both commitment and accessibility to collaborative research. The Centre for British Studies offers the chance to achieve this objective, which is to approach the culture of Great Britain through a network of interlocking disciplines.

By thematizing culture, the humanities regain their focus – a focus they lost when 'reified fundamentals' such as spirit, nation, personality formation, and the storage of the past were rampant. Growing discontent with such orientations had quickly resulted in attempts to expand the field of academic activities, as reflected for instance in the establishment of comparative studies as a discipline. Comparative approaches, however, be it to literature or history, suffered early on from a lack of answers to the basic question why one thing ought to be compared to another. In the final analysis, comparison turned out to be an empty category, at best testifying to some unspecified need to make up for the lost orientation of the humanities. Approaches to culture under the auspices of area studies [*Kulturkunde*], usually practised by those who had neither expertise nor competence in any of the established disciplines, moved in the same direction. Therefore, any responsible attempt to thematize culture will have to call both for institutionalized inter-disciplinarity and for a dialogue between participating disciplines that must be willing to take certain risks.

For interdisciplinarity will inevitably cause a given discipline to cross its traditional boundaries, but this must never mean subjecting the disciplinary core to amateurism; instead, each participating discipline must play its own specialized part in an undertaking that will carry it beyond its own established practices. In other words, whenever the disciplines of history, literature, linguistics, political science, law, and economics join forces in order to investigate culture, their interaction will result in insights that were previously not in their orbits. By entertaining the risks that are part and parcel of such cross overs, the disciplines may find themselves exposed to an experience of the cultural circulation which actually shapes their own cognitive acts.

For culture is not a unified, let alone a monolithic entity. Instead, it may be more accurately described as a plurality of legal, economic, and political systems as well as those of the arts, the media, etc. which permanently interact with one another. Various levels of high culture and subculture, minority and popular culture may come to the fore, or work away in the background. However, the plurality of systems, the stratification of levels (relative to an observer), their constant interaction as well as the dynamic transmission of information form only the prevalent frames of reference for culture, without ever allowing any fixed concept of what it may be.

The impossibility of pin-pointing the foundations of culture ought to encourage the collaborating disciplines to make life in a particular culture comprehensible. One could generalize by saying that culture appears to a given observer as a permanently self-organizing system.[15] The same holds true even of its components, no matter whether they refer to specific systems or to the various levels which in the course or their interaction always cause perturbations that in turn have to be processed. Such perturbations force the systems to restructure themselves, thereby altering their internal relationships. These changes manifest themselves as permanent feedbacks, which cause the systems to process perturbations, and hence continually to specify relationships.

Feedback also interlocks all levels of culture in the form of reciprocal intervention. Subculture, for instance, undercuts hegemonic structures of evaluation, and high culture marginalizes such acts of subversion. Minority culture exploits high culture, and the latter turns ethnic cultures into exhibits. These cultural levels form relations among one another – just as systems do – by permanently circulating information that is channelled through recursive loops. These feedback loops reveal the fact that culture not only shapes and reshapes itself as a result of its components' transformation, but also periodically transcends the existing configurations of its components in order to generate new ones in the process of cultural circulation. Culture is an 'emergence,' in the sense that it emerges as that which exceeds the configurations of its components.

Revealing the complexities of this process is a task that lies well beyond the boundaries of a single discipline; it requires interdisciplinarity, and it was this requirement that determined the guidelines for establishing the various chairs in the Centre for British Studies.[16]

Such area-oriented professorships have a twofold function to fulfil: they should represent a discipline, and simultaneously cover crucial components of British culture. Thus, they refer to literature and art; to legal, economic, and social systems; to the historical processes of modernization; to comparative government with respect to the European Union; to the semiotic systems of cultures and the media; and finally to the impact Great Britain has had on the non-European world.

This blueprint denotes an institutional response to the pressure of legitimization to which the humanities have found themselves exposed. As the different areas are linked to various cultural components, they are intended to bind together the hitherto fragmented and all too specialized humanities. Instead of falling back on special interests that no longer find public acceptance, they not only allow the humanities and social sciences to join up, but these in turn are 'open also to integrate the natural sciences, which only come into existence, and can only be comprehended, in their cultural context'.[17]

Furthermore, this multi-faceted approach to culture will give focus to collaborative research among the area-oriented professorships. Such cooperation will inevitably have repercussions on the way in which the components of each area are processed, so that their underlying assumptions will be exposed to change. Hence a culture-related collaboration between academic disciplines may be said to operate according to a feedback loop similar to that which structures the self-organization of culture itself. The interdisciplinary subject matter to be thematized thus constitutes the very parameters within which collaborative research is designed to develop.

Whenever culture is understood as a plurality of systems and a stratification of various levels (relative to an observer) which respond to one another by exchanging information or by interpenetration, the disciplines joined in a study of culture will no longer invoke any overriding paradigm, as was the case with literature in the past. For culture cannot be reduced to any of its components; instead, their structural coupling unfolds in a process that in turn generates components such as the media industry and then reshuffles the flow of information and subsequently affects the self-organization of culture. Members of the Centre who join in collaborative research will have to focus on these processes which transform and reshape culture itself.

Great Britain serves as an outstanding example of this interplay of systems and levels of cultures. The inroads of Norman into Anglo-Saxon culture led to Britain's medieval culture, which in turn became regionalized through the Irish, Scots, and Welsh, split into a society of two nations during the Industrial Revolution, and finally unfolded its modernity through the prevalent multiculturalism of our time. Moreover, the impact of British national culture exercised on the non-European world led to encounters that created Anglophone cultures, which in turn diversified cross-cultural relationships in hitherto inconceivable directions.[18]

The study of these relations as processes of mutual accommodation, appropriation, and translation will be a basic objective to be tackled jointly by the various disciplines of the Centre. Perhaps it is more than just a historical coincidence that Thomas Carlyle, in his theory laden narrative *Sartor Resartus* of 1836, provided a paradigm of how a reciprocal translation of cultures issues into cross-cultural discourse.[19] He transposed the concept-oriented philosophical culture of German idealism into the experience-oriented culture of British empiricism. If empirical criteria guide the takeover of German Transcendentalism, an alien set of references is applied that both dwarfs and enlarges features of Transcendentalism, while the same thing happens to Empiricism when Transcendentalism provides the criteria. Out of this blending arises a cross-cultural discourse, which does not, however, determine what a given culture is; instead, it makes each culture mirror the other, providing a kind of stage on which different cultures are enacted under alien conditions. It follows that neither culture can remain unchanged; as they refract one another, they both create something adumbrated by a phrase near the end of the novel: 'Es geht an' [*It begins*].[20]

Such a beginning may be conceived as an effort to comprehend otherness, which can only be grasped through a discourse that refrains from subjugating the foreign to the familiar. Of course, any such discourse will have to start out from the familiar; at the same time, however, its inevitable miscalculations with respect to the foreign will have to be fed back into its own assumptions. For a foreign culture becomes accessible to the extent that its observers modify their own preconceived notions about that culture. This reciprocal relation between foreign observers and foreign cultures plays itself out in the form of a feedback loop, in which insufficient input returns as revised output that feeds as fine-tuning into subsequent inputs. A discourse of this kind is in sync with the recursive interaction operative between systems as components of culture, as well as with the interplay between cultural levels (relative to observers), and the reciprocal invasion of cultures foreign to one another.

In order to develop such a discourse, the area-oriented disciplines of the Centre must needs work in close co-operation. Since culture can only be described, but not determined – for there is no external vantage point that would allow the disciplines to identify what it is – a framework for its description is an absolute necessity. Such a framework can only be devised through the boundary-crossing of interdisciplinarity, as only collaborating disciplines can track the reciprocal intervention of cultural systems, the interplay of cultural levels (relative to an observer), and the translatability of foreign cultures. This undertaking is basic to the study of culture, since the life of a culture to be assessed will be identical neither to its components nor to the processes triggered by them. Simultaneously, however, this basic research has a practical application,[21] inasmuch as the process of European integration has created a demand for specialists with cultural competence.

Thus the application-related basic research to be conducted in the Centre for British Studies will make it possible to reintegrate what has become divorced in the development of the humanities during the twentieth century in Germany: concerns both with the foundation of knowledge and with its practical utilization. Therefore, the research in the Centre will no longer be separated from its application, nor will it be subjected to purely practical interests. A study of culture through multidisciplinary collaboration will override restrictions entailed in the traditional opposition between education [*Bildung*] and vocational training [*Ausbildung*]. Whoever studies at the Centre will be introduced to the complex configurations of cultures and will learn to comprehend the structure of interactions between the systems, the levels (relative to an observer), and the political, economic, legal, medial, and æsthetic components, and will therefore have certain major advantages on the job market.

Graduates of the Centre for British Studies will be qualified to find work in the public sector – for instance in departments of cultural affairs, in the media, in the public relations organizations of German and British corporations, in the European institutions, and in the economic sector. While putting their knowledge into practice, however, they will also bring to bear a certain consciousness of culture in terms of the context encompassing their professions, for their studies will have taught them to examine culture through the network of its components. If in our secularized world culture has turned into the only fathomable manifestation of humans, professionals that have graduated from the Centre will bear in mind that their occupational practice is only a segment and not a whole.

The Centre for British Studies is an experiment which has every chance for success. The latter is eminently desirable, not least because it may rescue the humanities from the marginality in which they are presently deadlocked. Institutional pressure for the participating disciplines to engage in collaborative research and team-teaching promises to do just that. There is symbolic value in establishing a regional institute intended to reform humanistic studies at the very university that was founded by Wilhelm von Humboldt. Let us hope the concept of the Centre for British Studies will thrive in the spirit of Humboldt by giving new shape and new life to the humanities.

The lecture was delivered in German and published under the title *Das Großbritannien Zentrum in kulturwissenschaftlicher Sicht* (Öffentliche Vorlesungen der Humboldt-Universität Berlin, Heft, 53), Berlin 1995, pp. 21.

NOTES

1. Resolution 5502/95 passed by the Senate of Berlin, January 17, 1995.
2. Ibid.
3. See Michael Kahn, *Kunst der Überlistung. Studien zur Wissenschaftsgeschichte der Rhetorik* (Theorie und Geschichte der Literatur und der Schönen Künste, 76), Munich: Fink. 1986, pp. 107-147.
4. For details see my essay "Anglistik. Eine Universitätsdisziplin ohne Forschungsparadigma", in: *Poetica,* 16 (1984), pp. 279ff.
5. Wolfgang Frühwald, "Humanistische und naturwissenschaftlich-technische Bildung: die Erfahrung des 19. Jahrhunderts", in: Wolfgang Frühwald *et al., Geisteswissenschaft heute. Eine Denkschrift*, Frankfurt/M.: Suhrkamp (stw 973), 1991, p. 100.
6. Ibid.
7. H.-U. Gumbrecht, '"Un souffle d'Allemagne ayant passe.' Friedrich Diez, Gaston Paris und die Genese der Neuphilologien," in: W. Haubrichs and G. Sander (eds.), *Wissenschaftsgeschichte der Philologien*, Göttingen 1984, pp. 37-87.
8. For details see my essay *Das Literaturverständnis zwischen Geschichte und Zukunft* (Aulavorträge, 10), St. Gallen, 1981, pp. 13-16.
9. See Odo Marquard, *Apologie des Zufälligen*, Stuttgart 1986, pp. 98-116.
10. See Ernst Tugendhat, *Die Geisteswissenschaften als Aufklärungswissenschaften*, Manuscript, 1989.
11. See C.P. Snow, *The Two Cultures and the Scientific Revolution*, Cambridge University Press, 1959.
12. Jürgen Mittelstraß, "Die Geisteswissenschaften im System der Wissenschaft", in: *Geisteswissenschaften heute*, loc. cit., p. 27.
13. Clifford Geertz, *The Interpretation of Cultures: Selected Essays,* New York: Basic Books, 1973, p. 36.
14. Ibid., p. 42.
15. See William R. Paulson, *The Noise of Culture. Literary Texts in a World of Information,* Ithaca and London, 1988, pp. 53-100.
16. See "Empfehlungen des Gründungsauschusses für das Großbritannien-Zentrum an der Humboldt Universität zu Berlin", in Rüdiger Ahrens (ed.), *Anglistik. Organ des Verbandes Deutscher Anglisten,* 5 (1994), p. 11.
17. Reinhart Koselleck, "Wie sozial ist der Geist der Wissenschaften? Zur Abgrenzung der Sozial und Geisteswissenschaften", in: *Geisteswissenschaften heute,* loc. cit., p. 139.
18. For details see my outline for the design of a Centre for British

Studies at the Humboldt University, Berlin (Manuscript 1991), which formed the basis of the discussion held by the committee for the foundation of the Centre.

19. For details see my essay "The Emergence of a Cross Cultural Discourse: Thomas Carlyle's *Sartor Resartus*", in: Sanford Budick and Wolfgang Iser (eds.), *The Translatability of Cultures. Figurations of the Space Between*, Stanford, 1996, pp. 246-265.

20. Thomas Carlyle, *Sartor Resartus. The Life and Opinions of Herr Teufelsdröckh*, London: Centenary Edition, vol. I, 1897, p. 236.

21. See Jürgen Mittelstraß, "Zukunft Forschung. Perspektiven der Hochschulforschung in einer Leonardo-Welt", in: *Essener Hochschulblätter,* 1990, pp. 15-41, esp. p. 32.

EUREKA:
THE INTERPRETATION OF *TOM JONES*
Some Remarks Concerning Interpretation

Lothar Cerny's essay on "Reader Participation and Rationalism in *Tom Jones*"[1] has triggered a lively discussion, to which Bernard Harrison[2] and Leona Toker[3] have made substantial contributions. As some of my statements regarding reader-response have been focused on and indeed attacked in this debate, it may not be inappropriate to highlight the implications of Cerny's claim that he knows what Fielding really meant when using the word 'sagacity' in *Tom Jones*. Although 'sagacity' is differently contextualized in Fielding's novel – to which Leona Toker has drawn attention[4] – it nevertheless has a fixed meaning for Cerny, and he sticks to this assertion in spite of the fact that he once quotes Wittgenstein, from whom he might have learned that the meaning of a word is its use which, of course, varies. Shades of meaning, however, are not Cerny's concern, perhaps because they might subvert his claim to know exactly what was in

Fielding's mind.

Such a type of interpretation calls for scrutiny, and as I do not want to provide another interpretation of *Tom Jones*, I should like to raise a couple of issues that seem to have been overlooked in Cerny's essay: namely, why interpretation is frequently a matter of dispute, and what the difference is between methods of interpretation and theory.

Every interpretation transposes something into a different register that is not part of the subject matter to be interpreted. Therefore, each interpretation is an act of translation, in the course of which something is shifted into what it is not. In the case under discussion, a literary text is translated into a cognitive discourse, which makes any such act into a two-tiered operation. The literary discourse is the subject matter, and the cognitive discourse provides the parameters within which it is to be understood.

Comprehending *Tom Jones* could be directed towards ascertaining what the novel is about, what it means, what it intends, what it represents, what impact it exercises, what responses it elicits, what its representation aims at, and so on. There is a wide potential range of registers into which the literary discourse may be translated. Such a two-tiered operation brings the inherent duality of the register to the fore. All the viewpoints listed – and one can think of many more – decide what is important for the respective interpretation. As the viewpoints are selective, they give each interpretation a particular slant. The problem, however, is that the cognitive terms of the register are partial, and so the register actually molds the subject matter to the shape of its own interest.

This inherent duality makes it impossible to claim full knowledge of the text to be interpreted. Hence any such claim can only mean – in the case under consideration – to identify *Tom Jones* with the stance adopted for grasping the novel. This is strikingly illustrated by what Cerny claims to have found – namely, the intention Fielding is supposed to have pursued in *Tom Jones*, summed up by the statement: 'Just as he expresses his belief in a dialectical unity of erotic love and charity, he equally looks to the unity of reason and feeling in wisdom.' (157) How can 'unity' be the guiding intention of someone who announces in his 'Bill of Fare to the Feast' that the 'Provision' for him 'is no other than H U M A N N A T U R E,' whose importance is emphasized by spaced capital letters, and which is of 'such prodigious Variety, that a Cook will have sooner gone through all the several Species of animal and vegetable Food in the World, than an author will be able to exhaust so extensive a Subject.'"[5]

Interpretation is bound to go awry when the following considerations are not sufficiently heeded: First, the ineluctable partiality of the terms set by the register, and second – even more importantly – the space opened up by any act of interpretation between the subject matter and the register into which the latter is transposed. This space cannot be ignored, but has to be negotiated, otherwise the inherent stances of the cognitive discourse are just superimposed on the literary discourse. Now, Cerny's claim that 'unity' is to be considered the hallmark of human nature clearly shows the partiality of his interpretation: a set of assumptions is elevated to the status of reality. Negotiation, however, implies going back and forth between one's assumptions and the text, thus developing a hermeneutic circularity that acknowledges the space opened up by any interpretation, and simultaneously brings under scrutiny one's assumptions which, when focused upon, will not stay the same.

This is almost exactly the kind of repair that Harrison carries out on Cerny's claim to know that Fielding strove for 'unity'; he highlights the interplay between 'Reason' and 'Appetite', whose oxymoronic relationship – according to Harrison – Fielding unfolds in kaleidoscopically shifting patterns, which both shatter and rebuild reader expectations. 'He has constructed, with extreme detail and verisimilitude, an array of cases in which Appetite wields the sceptre of Principle, passion turns out to lie at the heart of goodness, morality turns out to demand worldliness (in a certain sense) of us, and unworldliness (in a certain sense) stands under moral condemnation. All this may indeed stagger the reader; but if it does, the expectations it staggers are not introduced for the first time to the reader through his hermeneutic struggles with the text, but ones insinuated by presumptions, fore-understandings, which while they are not, in fact, essential to the preservation of a common understanding of terms in the language in which the text is written, are sufficiently engrained and habitual within the cultural milieu addressed by the text as to seem so.' (162)

In the final analysis, a claim to knowledge is alien to interpretation, which would be redundant if one knew the 'true' nature of the matter to be explored. For interpretation is an attempt to understand what is beyond knowing. Therefore negotiation is the guiding principle of interpretation, not least because any claim to knowing colonizes the very space between object and register that interpretation itself has opened up.

Why should someone who 'knows' what Fielding's enterprise was, deem it necessary to debunk the statements of those who are not in line with his thinking? Why should he pay any attention at all to those who are wrong, especially if he 'knows' that they started out from false presuppositions anyway, and thus were bound to go astray?

Well, no premise of interpretation is self-evident in view of what it is meant to achieve. The short cut to justifying one's own premise, therefore, is to single out opponents and tear them to pieces, implying, of course, that this is already sufficient evidence for the validity of one's own assumptions. The more vehement the attack, the more the assumptions depend on constant reminders of the opponent's failure. If the opponent has to be caricatured to the verge of simple-mindedness, the effect can only be to divert attention from the premise on which the attack is based. It is, after all, no proof of strength to say that the position attacked is weak.

Cerny's interpretive strategies make one thing quite clear: he does not consider his premise to be a heuristic assumption; assumptions initiate and develop trial runs, and since they can never cover all eventualities, some of their features must be exposed to change. Furthermore, Cerny does not reflect on what is inherent in his premise – and why should he, in view of his certainty that he is right? Such an attitude is sadly reminiscent of those outmoded brands of explanation which laid claim to a monopoly on interpretation. The proponents of such claims inspected only other people's premises, but never their own, which for them had a self-proclaimed authority. However, they too were dependent on opponents, whose different starting-points had to be distorted in order to provide negative support for the would-be indisputable.

I have obviously also been tailored in such a manner, and thereby converted into a foundational element of Cerny's interpretive enterprise. That he needs me urgently is borne out by the fact that even when replying to Harrison's criticism, he calls me up as his whipping-boy. It is flattering to be so indispensable, though a little disconcerting to be seen as simple-minded. I am used to my work being regarded as too abstract, sometimes too difficult, even too complicated, but now suddenly, according to Cerny, it is simplistic: 'In his attempt to establish a place for reader participation, Iser knows only one alternative, either didacticism or vacant spaces, tertium non datur.' (143)[6] If only I had known this earlier, I could have saved myself hundreds of pages.

My Cernyian mask of simplicity did not last long, as both Bernard Harrison and Leona Toker swiftly pulled it off. Harrison explained very succinctly the phenomenologically conceived text processing that I had advanced, and even stressed the fact that in the reading process the 'noetic-noematic constitution' requires a 'continuous adjustment of anticipations in the light of their fulfilment.' (150) Of course, this adjustment will apply to the text-processing of *Tom Jones*, as each reader brings different anticipations to bear, just as each interpreter has preferences for his or her chosen assumptions. Cerny bridles at this, and begins his rebuttal of Harrison's criticism by stating: 'He (Harrison) has given us, in fact, a theory of reader-response which he, rather too modestly, claims to be a modification of Iser's theory only.'[7] Well, why not? And isn't modification integral to our common pursuit of exploring issues and addressing problems in literary criticism? At least it is more productive than the currently fashionable victimary discourse.

Leona Toker has given an exhaustive analysis of my attempts to conceptualize the different *lacunæ* in the text, thus providing an impressive demonstration of why the register of any interpretation should be examined first, as it forestalls a rush to judgment in the conflict of interpretation. 'Reading the Instructions' – as she puts it – means inspecting the register into which the subject matter is translated. Such an inspection is all the more pertinent as the register not only molds the subject matter, but also translates it into a contemporary context. In other words, the register is conditioned by the context out of which it has arisen, and its fashioning of the subject matter is essential if the latter is to be translated into terms of contemporary understanding. In the two-tiered structure of interpretation, the register itself is dual by nature, as it simultaneously gives a perspective to the subject matter, and transmits it into the parameters of a particular intellectual environment.

This is a basic reason why interpretation has to come under scrutiny. For a long time, it was just an activity carried out without much attention to what it actually entailed. It was tacitly assumed that interpretation was something that came naturally, not least as human beings live by constantly interpreting. However, what does not come naturally are the forms interpretation takes. And as these forms structure the acts of interpretation to a large extent, it is important to study them, not least as the structures will reveal what the respective interpretive agenda is designed to achieve.

This is all the more essential with a prevailing type of interpretation that predicates and judges what in actual fact has to be understood. Understanding entails opening up the issues to be explored, whereas predication and judgment provide closure, thus pointing to a transcendental stance which decrees what the subject matter has to be. The critic, however, as T.S. Eliot once remarked, 'must not coerce, and he must not make judgments of worse or better. He must simply elucidate: the reader will form the correct judgment for himself.'[8] Otherwise, we might add, interpretation is merely decision-making, and as such stands in need of deconstruction, since it reifies either individual or contingent preferences, which more often than not block the road to an historically and situationally conditioned understanding.

There is a final point to be touched upon briefly: the distinction between method and theory of which, to put it mildly, Cerny seems unaware in his magisterial interpretation. He starts out his first essay by saying: 'Fielding's novels, therefore, do not just serve Iser as examples to illustrate his theory but actually provide the patterns or substrata on which it is based.' (137) And he has another dig at me in his second essay, maintaining that 'a theory' cannot 'be convincing which does not really meet its chosen empirical subject.' (314) Irrespective of whether a theory is convincing or not, it is certainly not a method of interpretation.

In the past I have already tried to explain the difference between theory and method, and for argument's sake, I am afraid I have to quote myself: 'Theories generally provide premises, which lay the foundation for the framework of categories, whereas methods provide the tools for processes of interpretation. Thus the phenomenological theory, for instance, explores the mode of existence of the artwork; the hermeneutic theory is concerned with the observer's understanding of himself when confronted with the work; the gestalt theory focuses on the perceptive faculties of the observer as brought into play by the work. (...) Distinctive assumptions are made which reveal a particular mode of access to the work of art, although they do not represent a technique of interpretation. Theories must undergo a definite transformation if they are to function as interpretative techniques. Thus the bases laid down by the three theories above must be transformed into (a) the strata model, (b) question and answer logic, and (c) the concepts of schema and correction. There is, in fact, a hermeneutic relationship between theory and method. Every theory embodies an abstraction of the material it is seeking to categorize. If the degree of abstraction is the precondition for the success of categorization, then, clearly, the theory tends to screen off the individuality of the material, whereas it is the central function of interpretative methods to bring out and elucidate this very individuality. Thus the theory provides a frame-work of categories, while the method, in turn, provides the conditions whereby the basic assumptions underlying the theory will be differentiated by the results emerging from individual analysis.'[9]

A theory of æsthetic response, as I tried to conceive it, follows the very same lines, i.e. it has to be transformed, if a method of interpretation is to be derived from it.[10] However, when a theory is taken for a method of interpretation, either confusion or redundancy ensue: confusion insofar as the comparatively abstract frameworks of a theory tend to distort the text when used as guidelines for interpretation; redundancy insofar as texts are turned into documentation when used to bear out a theory that really does not need such evidence. In each instance, the hermeneutic interrelationship between theory and method is lost to view. If theory furnishes the focus for a method, the latter in turn can feed its findings back into the theory, which is thus fine-tuned.

At a historic juncture in literary studies, this circularity became paramount in order to dispel the smokescreen arising from an impressionistic type of interpretation that took the emotion aroused by the art work for its intrinsic structure. This is reason enough for observing the distinction between theory and method, and this is exactly what Leona Toker has stressed in her contribution, to which, by way of conclusion, I can unreservedly subscribe. 'A literary example can partially illustrate but not bear out a theory, since, as noted above, a literary text is a testing ground rather than a tribune for ideas, a field which only partly overlaps with the theory one superimposes on it. It is richer than a theory in some ways and poorer in others (less numerous); and it will necessarily indicate the insufficiencies of this theory while failing to do justice to its extensions.' (160)

NOTES

1. *Connotations,* 2 (1992), pp. 137-162

2. Bernard Harrison, "Gaps and Stumbling Blocks in Fielding: A Response to Cerny, Hammond and Hudson", *Connotations,* 3 (1993/94), pp. 147-172.

3. Leona Toker, "If Everything Else Fails, Read the Instructions: Further Echoes of the Reception Theory Debate", *Connotations,* 4 (1994/95), pp. 151-164.

4. Cf. ibid., p. 154-6.

5. Henry Fielding, *The History of Tom Jones, A Foundling,* I (The Wesleyan Edition of the Works of Henry Fielding), ed. by Fredson Bowers, Oxford University Press, 1975, pp. 31f.

6. Cerny's way of arguing can be illustrated by just one example. He tries to highlight one of my many failures by quoting the following passage: 'This typical appeal to the reader's 'sagacity' aims at arousing a sense of discernment… Here we have a clear outline of the role of the reader, which is fulfilled through the continual instigation of attitudes and reflections on those attitudes." Cerny takes this statement to be yet another indication of my blindness. But then on the opposite page, with my own quote still in view, he writes: 'Fielding does not altogether dispense with teaching. On the contrary, he wants to teach in a less obvious and more effective way. He makes the reader learn on his own, not by telling him what he thinks is right but by letting him discover sense and nonsense for himself.' (143)

7. Lothar Cerny, "'But the poet…never affirmeth': A Reply to Bernard Harrison", *Connotations,* 3, (1993/94), p. 312.

8. T. S. Eliot, "The Perfect Critic", in *The Sacred Wood. Essays on Poetry and Criticism,* London, 1960, p. 11; the essay was originally published in 1928.

9. Wolfgang Iser, "The Current Situation of Literary Theory: Key Concepts and the Imaginary", *New Literary History* 11 (1979), p. 5. It should be added that theories are also conceived to explore issues which may not have anything to do with providing parameters for interpreting literary texts, such as those which focus on the function of literature, or on what literature may reveal of the human makeup.

10. I have tried to make such a transformation myself in my book on *Shakespeares Historien. Genesis und Geltung,* Konstanz 1988; but I certainly did not do so in my essay on Fielding.

INTERVIEW
(1984)

Conducted by Nabila Salem Ibrahim

NABILA SALEM IBRAHIM: How could we interpret texts with your theory and what are prominent theories in Germany to day?

WOLFGANG ISER: First of all, I should like to make a distinction which is frequently blurred in the discussion of literary theories and methods. More often than not the terms theory and method are used as if they were similar or even interchangeable, but there are important differences.

Theories generally provide premises for a framework of categories, whereas methods provide tools for processes of interpretation. Theories must undergo a definite transformation if they are to function as interpretive techniques, so that in fact there is a hermeneutic relationship operative between theory and method. Every theory embodies an abstraction of the material it is seeking to categorize. If the degree of abstraction is the precondition for the success of categorization, then clearly the theory tends to screen off the individuality of the material, whereas it is the central function of interpretive methods to bring out and elucidate this very individuality. Thus the theory provides a frame-work of categories, while the method enables the basic assumptions underlying the theory to be differentiated through the results of individual analysis.

This basic difference is frequently overlooked, and if theory is used as if it were an interpretive method, the resultant difficulties lead either to confusion or to complaints that the theory does not work as a method.

Currently the following theories are making an impact on the German intellectual scene: Marxism, Analytical Language Theory, Information Theory, Hermeneutics and Psychoanalysis. For literary studies in particular, Marxism, Psychoanalysis and Hermeneutics are prominent, but an empirical theory of literature has also gained ground in recent years. Its main task is to register people's responses and to draw inferences concerning the social code governing their attitudes.

Prior to the impact exercised by the above-mentioned theories, New Criticism was rampant in German literary studies, as it constituted a reaction to a utilization of the literary text for many different, especially political, purposes in Germany's recent past.

NABILA SALEM IBRAHIM: In which way did your reader response theory arise out of the situation that you have just described?

WOLFGANG ISER: The arguments set out in my two books *The Implied Reader* and *The Act of Reading* were conceived as a reaction not to current modern theories, but rather to something which had previously been neglected in literary studies: the reader. After all, literature is written in order to be read, and to elicit a response from its potential reader. This area of literary studies was relatively uncharted, and so in the late sixties the so-called Konstanz School set out to explore the field.

Reader-response criticism and æsthetics of reception were not, then, an attack on current literary theories and methods, but a counterbalance to the interest focused solely on the text and on the author respectively. For this reason, reception theory conceived of the text in terms of a process, i.e. an interrelation between author, text, and reader, and tried to devise a framework in order to assess this inter-relationship.

At the time when these ideas were put forward, Post-Structuralism was not very prominent, and Deconstruction had not caught on in the field of literary studies. Furthermore, one could hardly say that æsthetics of reception and reader-response criticism are a continuation of any particular trend in German philosophical thought. If they have to be linked to certain tenets prevailing in German philosophy, then their closest affiliation is to Hermeneutics and Phenomenology. The phenomenological theory explores the mode of existence of the art work, while hermeneutic theories are concerned with the observer's understanding of himself or herself when confronted with the work. In that respect, certain ideas current in the twenties were appropriated as starting-points for the theories in question.

NABILA SALEM IBRAHIM: Could you give a description of the relationship of your work to the phenomenological tenets you have just mentioned, and to what extent did you develop a phenomenologically-oriented theory of reader-response out of it?

WOLFGANG ISER: A Phenomenological Theory of Art lays full stress on the idea that, in considering a literary work, one must take into account not only the actual text but also, and in equal measure, the actions involved in responding to it. Thus

Roman Ingarden, who had been a student of Edmund Husserl's, confronts the structure of the literary text with the way in which it can be realized. The text as such offers different schematized views through which the subject matter of the work can come to light, but the actual bringing to light is an act of 'concretization'.

This was the basic starting-point for my work, and although it is of course already a consequence to be derived from classical Phenomenology as put forward by Husserl, as a general idea it stood in need of extension and transformation. I have tried to do this from two angles of approach:

a) The literary work as mapped out in a Phenomenological Theory of Art may be said to have two poles, which we might call the artistic and the æsthetic: the artistic refers to the text created by the author, and the æsthetic to the realization accomplished by the reader. From this polarity it follows that the literary work cannot be completely identical with the text, or with its realization, but in fact must lie halfway between the two. The work is more than the text, for the text takes on life only when it is realized, and furthermore this realization is by no means independent of the individual disposition of the reader though the latter, in turn, is acted upon by the different patterns of the text. The convergence of text and reader brings the literary work into existence, and this convergence can never be precisely pinpointed, but must always remain virtual, as it is not to be identified either with the reality of the text or with the individual disposition of the reader. This intricate relationship stood in need of exploration, and I set out to investigate the reading process within which this interaction occurs, and out of which meaning is assembled as a product of this interaction.

b) If the literary text comes to life by being concretized in the reading process, then the process itself has to be conceived in terms of communication – an idea which was neglected in the phenomenological approach to art. Therefore I stressed the concept of structured blanks and gaps in the text which stimulate the combinatory faculty of the reader, thus engaging him or her in the processing of the text. Communication is not just a transfer from text to reader, but it is an interpretation of what the reader is given to tackle. I tried to put forward a theory of structured blanks in order to conceptualize literary communication.

NABILA SALEM IBRAHIM: Do you consider your theory superior to those that are linked more closely to classical æsthetics, and how would you describe the function your theory is meant to fulfil?

WOLFGANG ISER: There is no doubt that theories other than the one I put forward have merits of their own. In answer to your question, however, I would have to say that contemplation of the literary text is an offshoot of classical æsthetics, which in these days is generally regarded out of date. Walter Benjamin has convincingly criticised the aura of the literary work, and thus – at least for the time being – discredited the contemplative attitude towards the art work.

My concern with the work of art is not what it gives us to contemplate, or what it is supposed to mean, so much as what it does to us. For this reason I am primarily concerned with the function of the literary work, and there are not many current theories which try to assess this function in whatever terms. Marxism may be the only exception, but according to the inherent gnosticism of Marxist ideology, the function of literature appears to be highly predetermined. My aim, however, is to provide a framework which will allow for an evaluation of the changing functions of literature in varying historical contexts.

Therefore I have chosen General Systems Theory as a point of departure for the assessment of such a function. General Systems Theory does not concern itself with art, but tries to find the underlying pattern of all the various interpretations of life we usually call our reality. We move in different systems all the time, each one of which is differentiated by the norms and values that are prominent, that have a neutral character, and that are negated. This triadic inter-relationship of each system points to the fact that systems are problem-solving instruments, but each successful resolution of a problem is prone to produce new problems. It is to these deficiencies that literature addresses itself by undermining the system in order to show up its constituent elements or interests that underlie them, or alternatively by shoring up the system which is threatened by a new development in life. In this respect the function of literature can be subversive or stabilizing, and it will change according to historical necessities. Consequently literature functions as a means of divining, identifying and exploring the deficiencies in the patterns of our reality.

NABILA SALEM IBRAHIM: How can one interpret reality from the angle that you have outlined, and how does the reader arrive at or ascertain the meaning of the text?

WOLFGANG ISER: What I have just said ties in with your question. As each system is a form of interpretation, literature, by constantly making inroads into these systems, recodes them. In this respect each text is a reformulation of an already formulated reality. Through the recoding of existing patterns of reality something new comes into the world, and the literary text functions as a channel for this particular kind of innovation.

Moreover the text is also a set of instructions. It either provides information or invokes existing experiences, subjecting both to combinations and transformations by its unfolding strategies. In this manner the reader is manœuvred into a position to undergo the kind of experience the text intends to convey.

Now the kind of interpretation you are referring to appears to be a very intricate process, and it is necessary to distinguish between its various stages. If the reader is involved and thus participates in the constitution of the meaning, he or she will definitely encounter this meaning as a form of experience. Whenever we have an experience, we feel compelled to talk about it, i.e. we want to translate it into cognitive terms. Therefore I would like to distinguish between meaning and significance. Meaning is brought about by involving the reader in the act of its constitution; significance is attached to the meaning the moment it has been translated into cognition. The inevitable quest for significance shows that in assembling the meaning, we ourselves become aware that something has happened to us, and so we try to find out its significance. Meaning and significance are not the same; the significance of the meaning can only be ascertained when meaning is related to a particular reference which makes it translatable into familiar terms. There are two distinct stages that occur in the reading process: the stage of meaning assembly and the stage of significance, which represents the active taking over of the meaning by the reader, i.e. the meaning taking effect in the reader's existence.

NABILA SALEM IBRAHIM: I think there is a great difference between reading a text of the past or the present, and you seem to be more interested in texts of the past to which your model more adequately applies, not least as in older literature the reader has to conform more strictly to the patterns of the text.

WOLFGANG ISER: I do not think that I privilege texts of the past within the framework I have outlined. What you said surprises me, as I have in fact been accused by several critics of deriving my ideas from the experience of Modern Literature. Furthermore, I should like to correct the idea that the reader has to conform to the basic patterns of the reading process that I have mapped out. What I had intended to do was to give a phenomenological description of what happens in reading, and not to provide instructions as to how an ideal reader ought to read.

To come back to your initial point concerning the difference between reading a work of the past and reading a contemporary work, I should like to say that in terms of function, reading a work of the past allows us to reconstitute the historical context to which the work in question responded. We could conceive of the relation in terms of question and answer, or problem and solution. Consequently a work of art cannot be considered as a mirror reflection, but rather as an integral constituent of that very reality within which it was produced. Thus the work makes an important contribution to the idea of the historical situation which each of us has to reconstruct if we want to come to grips with it. And for this reason the work of art, in addressing itself to the deficiencies of the world-picture prevailing at its time of origin, forms an inalienable part of the view we are able to obtain of that particular historical situation.

As for the contemporary reader, the literary text moves him or her into a position to observe from the outside norms, values and orientations which guide him or her in ordinary life. By recoding these guidelines, the literary text holds them up for inspection, and thus opens up an insight into something in which we are otherwise inextricably entangled. This appears to me one of the prime functions of literature, and such insight is certainly a valuable experience, no matter what the individual reader does with it.

NABILA SALEM IBRAHIM: If literature has an exploratory function as you say, to what extent has your theory any anthropological implications, which either guide your scholastic concerns or which are even in the nature of an objective of your investigation? Furthermore, how does your theory relate to what Derrida has developed?

WOLFGANG ISER: My research is certainly motivated by an anthropological interest. So far I have been mainly concerned with the interaction between the text, the context of its production, and the reader who processes it. There are, however, other questions which arise simultaneously, such as, 'Why do we stand in need of fictions?' and I believe that literary criticism should be able to address these questions. If we were to explore them, we could certainly learn something about the human makeup, and for this reason I consider literature to be a very important means of understanding the way in which we use our imaginary faculty in our daily lives – a process of which literature may indeed be a paradigm. In pursuing this line of research, one might be able to establish an anthropology of literature which in the end would provide an answer to the question of why we have to extend ourselves beyond ourselves.

As to the final point you raised regarding Deconstruction, I would rather reserve judgment. An adequate answer would call for a whole essay. Derrida provided literary criticism – at least in the United States – with a different framework which enabled those who had been trained as New Critics to discard the old frame of reference based on classical æsthetics, to exchange it for something broader based on a modernist experience, but to continue as close readers. Paul de Man spoke of these deconstructionists as the closest of close readers.

The interview was conducted in English, and subsequently published in Arabic in *Fusul: Journal of Literary Criticism* 1 (1984), Cairo.

AN INTERVIEW WITH WOLFGANG ISER

Conducted by Shan Te-hsing
Academia Sinica, Taipei, Taiwan

FIRST PART

March 21, 1994

SHAN TE-HSING: Do you have any specific expectations for your first trip to Taiwan?

WOLFGANG ISER: Certainly, since I am going to experience a very rare exposure to what is for me a completely foreign culture. As you may know, Europeans, and Germans in particular, have great respect for Chinese culture, and therefore it is very exciting for me to encounter it for the first time. Short as my stay may be, I am fascinated to see what impact this foreign culture will have on me.

WOLFGANG ISER   STEPPING FORWARD

SHAN TE-HSING: May I borrow the title of your second lecture and ask: what kind of 'recursive looping' or 'cross-cultural relationship' do you expect from your interaction with the local audience?

WOLFGANG ISER: First of all, 'recursive looping' develops as an interchange between input and output, in the course of which a familiar projection is corrected to the extent to which it has failed to square with what it has targeted. Consequently, a dual correction occurs: the feed forward returns as an altered feedback loop which, in turn, feeds into a revised input. For a foreign culture to become comprehensible, there must be a change of attitude towards the familiar one. This opens up a means of relating cross-culturally.

SHAN TE-HSING: Can you say something briefly about your lecture series and also explain a little the title of each lecture so that we can have a foretaste of what you are going to present here in Taiwan.

WOLFGANG ISER: Well, in the humanities the question of interpretation is of prime concern, because it is a constant and unavoidable activity. For this reason, I think it is time to inspect what we actually do when we interpret. Whenever we interpret something, we translate it into another register. Obviously, there are many different modes of translation, but in all cases, when you translate something into something else, that very act is bound to generate untranslatability. However, what cannot be transposed, or translated, energizes the very act of interpretation. So what I actually want to do in the three lectures is to find out how we negotiate the space opened up between what is to be interpreted and the register into which it is transposed. If 'authority' is brought to bear, the space between is eliminated, because authority colonizes it. If the space is bridged for the purpose of understanding what is interpreted, then it has to be negotiated by a circular movement. This applies basically to an understanding of texts.

But when we have to interpret a culture, for instance, which is not a text in the limited sense of the term, interpretation entails intervention into that culture, which is bound to react, whereas a text does not respond. The text does not 'talk back' to you, whereas a culture may well do so. Consequently, it is the space between the known and the unknown that has to be crossed.

My final example will deal with the question of what happens when something immeasurable, like God, the world, or humankind has to be or is translated into terms of cognition. In such cases the space between is of a different nature, and we must carry an immeasurable potential across into finite terms.

This will be the main thrust of my three lectures, which can be summed up by stating that each interpretation is a) an act of translation; b) dependent on the subject matter to be translated into another register; and c) dependent on the way in which the space opened up by any interpretation is dealt with.

The first lecture tries to provide a historical panorama starting out from the question: what conditions led to the rise of interpretation? It arose from the Judaic tradition of reading the canon (the sacred texts), in the course of which the authority of the canon shifted to the reading of it. I shall also investigate an example from the literary canon: Dr Johnson's reading of Shakespeare, who – as a canonical author – was appropriated by Dr Johnson to authenticate his own ideas. Such an appropriation marked a situation where the canon in the received sense was on the wane and hermeneutics on the rise. I shall unfold the hermeneutic tradition from Schleiermacher, who actually devised hermeneutics as a type of interpretation, right through to psychoanalysis.

In the second lecture, I shall use a piece of fiction, Thomas Carlyle's *Sartor Resartus*, which is one of the earliest paradigms to thematize a cross-cultural relationship. What Carlyle did, lends itself to generalization regarding cross-cultural interchange.

My final lecture will be devoted to the Jewish philosopher Franz Rosenzweig, who wanted to come to grips with the immeasurableness of God in epistemological terms, thus trying to achieve what Western philosophy was unable to do.

SHAN TE-HSING: How would you relate this series of lectures to your former intellectual career, such as your emphasis on interaction in *The Act of Reading*?

WOLFGANG ISER: A straightforward answer would be that it is my concern to investigate the enabling function of blanks. The space within each and every act of interpretation is a blank, so that there are blanks not only in texts but also in translation, in cross-cultural relationships, and between incommensurables and our attempts to grasp them. Perhaps these blanks are not only different from those in texts, but are even more important for what has to be coped with. In this respect, with the lectures I am going to give, my basic concerns broaden out into interpretation.

SHAN TE-HSING: How would you relate it to your concept of literary anthropology?

WOLFGANG ISER: It relates to questions of anthropology insofar as no translation can ever be total. Consequently, we as 'interpreting animals' – because whatever we do, even when raising our hands or eyebrows, is already an act of interpretation – constantly translate something into something else, be it in order to comprehend ('comprehension' in the sense of 'encompassing,' and 'embracing'), or to achieve more than was possible before. Yet we simultaneously realize that total translatability is impossible. Therefore, interpretation reveals something of the human condition, as we never stop interpreting in spite of our awareness that, in the final analysis, there is always something that cannot be transposed into a different register. The very unattainability of total translation does not induce human beings to let go. Consequently, we hang between the very possibilities we try out when we interpret, and hanging between may be the hallmark of the human condition.

SHAN TE-HSING: Can your new book *Staging Politics* be seen as your response to politicizing art or æstheticizing politics?

WOLFGANG ISER: No, I did not mean it that way, because it concerns itself basically with Shakespeare's *Histories*. My idea behind the book is as follows: when the medieval world order was on the wane, human beings lacked guidelines as to how they could accommodate themselves in a world that had not been tailored to their needs. Having to find their way in such a world, human beings embarked on politics, since politics is a form of human action which basically is pragmatically oriented. Consequently, the waning order gave birth to politics, and Shakespeare was one of the first to enact politics by exposing its possibilities and entrapments. Since politics on the threshold of the modern age marked a turning point in human affairs in the West, Shakespeare provided patterns of politics, which exhibited basic dispositions of human behaviour.

SHAN TE-HSING: How about the reception of this new book?

WOLFGANG ISER: The German version was comparatively well received, since it does not view literature as an opposition to politics, let alone an æstheticization of politics. The English version is just about to appear, and it will take some time before there is a response.

Obviously, politics as it manifested itself on the threshold of the modern age was a means of showing how human self-assertion and self-preservation could be organized and achieved in a world which, according to the Judaic-Christian tradition, was not actually meant for the sustenance of human beings, but was destined to perish. However, as this very world still persisted fifteen hundred years after Christ's resurrection, human beings had to accommodate themselves in it, and that meant they had to assert themselves by shaping it for their own ends. Such a situation accounts for the rise of politics at the inception of the modern age.

SHAN TE-HSING: How about the reception of *The Fictive and the Imaginary*?

WOLFGANG ISER: As you know, it always takes a while before a general statement made in a book filters down. Some people found it astonishing that one could make a distinction between the fictive and the imaginary, as these are generally regarded as interchangeable. The most positive response so far has been to the function of literature as it is mapped out in the book. What appears to be of great interest is my attempt to answer the question why human beings need fictions.

SHAN TE-HSING: Would you like to say something about your seminar as well as its topic "Growing up as an intellectual in postwar Germany"?

WOLFGANG ISER: I wouldn't really want to talk too much about myself. At best I consider myself a representative of a generation of schoolboys that were conscripted into the army towards the end of the Second World War, and then all of a sudden found themselves in a situation in which they had to sort themselves out. In order to do so, I studied literature and philosophy which, according to a European bourgeois tradition, were considered to be the best means of educating oneself and in those days meant coming to grips with oneself. However, the end of the war created a situation in which liberation and restoration meant the same thing, as a result of which we were trained as philologists along totally traditional lines. In other words, we were subjected to the repetition of ideas which were current in the twenties, but were now completely out of date. For instance, whenever the name of de Saussure was mentioned – which was hardly ever the case – it was made clear to us as students that someone who had advanced a synchronic system of language must have been out of his mind. Thus, a Chinese Wall – as we were inclined to say later on – was built against modernity in our student days in the late forties. Small wonder that when I went to Great Britain in the early fifties, after having completed my Ph.D., I was totally ignorant, and only gradually did it dawn on me that the modern world had happened.

SHAN TE-HSING: You and Professor Murray Krieger initiated the "International Centre for Humanistic Discourse (ICHD)."" Would you like to say something about this "Centre" and also its relationship to your project?

WOLFGANG ISER: I have reservations about calling it a "Centre." We struck a sort of compromise by saying it may be considered a centre as well as a conference. The letter 'C' in our acronym serves that purpose. But this is only a trivial point.

The humanities are under stress, and naturally this has repercussions on the profession. For this reason, we think it is time to look at the functions of the humanities in Europe, the United States, and in certain Asian cultures, such as China and

Japan. Simultaneously, we would like to ascertain the role of the arts in the formation of culture, to which they appear to be integral.

Such an enterprise relates to my own work insofar as both the humanities and the business of interpretation are in themselves cultural activities, embedded in a form which might be called humanistic discourse. Therefore the question arises as to how far the humanistic discourse influences the way in which the cultural heritage is transported from past into present, and to what extent it structures what is now called 'cultural studies' – a field which currently seems to be a free-for-all. 'Cultural studies' is a very basic concern of our time, given the shrinking distances and increasing contact between cultures, and therefore it is pertinent, in view of the prevailing confusion, that those engaged in that field should explain what they are doing.

Basically, I am inclined to say that the humanities exist in dialogue, since there is a continual interaction between what people say or do in relation to culture, and to art and literature in particular. For this reason a Humanities Research Institute which ignored such a dialogic relationship would get nowhere. Things are different in the natural sciences as they seek solutions to problems, whereas we relate to the cultural heritage, make it available, and try to feed it back into our present situation. Consequently, all of us who are engaged in such an activity should be in a permanent dialogue with one another, not least as past and present are similarly interlinked: we see ourselves reflected in the very past which we are trying to recover.

SHAN TE-HSING: Would you regard yourself, who travel around in different cultures and countries, as an agent in cross-cultural relationship?

WOLFGANG ISER: Although one is conditioned by the culture

to which one belongs, I nevertheless consider myself as someone who sits between cultures. This may also have something to do with my scholastic interest in the consequences of such an in-between state. What I generally do in Germany is bring an American experience to bear, trying to undo among other things the persistent clichés, and alerting my students to the multifarious intellectual activities of a culture continually on the move. When I am in the United States, I try to stress the importance of the historical sense – for which T.S. Eliot had already made a forceful plea quite some time ago – not least as history appears to be something external to American intellectual life. In this respect one functions as a self-appointed cross-cultural mediator.

SHAN TE-HSING: From what you have said, one gets the impression that you are not so politically alienated as you are sometimes taken to be as a scholar devoted to æsthetics.

WOLFGANG ISER: No, I am not politically alienated; I am even inclined to say that my interest in æsthetics has a political impulse. In a world in which so many appeals are made to human beings, from advertising to politics, many æsthetic devices are used in order to catch people's attention and to manipulate their perception. The impositions made on human beings in an ideology-ridden world need some kind of political illumination.

SHAN TE-HSING: So you are somewhat like Professor Murray Krieger, who tries to expose the pitfalls of the dominant ideologies by way of studying æsthetics?

WOLFGANG ISER: Although, as I have just said, there is a political impulse in my scholastic activities, I do not see the dichotomy between æsthetics and politics that is commonly assumed. This may be exemplified by what is currently called 'oppositional discourses', be it minority, anti-colonial, or feminist discourse, etc. People who advocate any such discourse more often than not maintain that everything is political. If you retort that this doesn't make sense, because something cannot be everything, they try to cut you short by saying: 'This Western junk logic is just another way of disciplining those who either reject or, even worse, oppose what the hegemonic discourse demands of them.' Such a situation – at least in my view – makes discourse analysis into a necessity. All the oppositional discourses we know of are basically politically oriented; but since they have none of the power which they attribute to the hegemonic discourse, it is absolutely necessary for them to be persuasive, otherwise they would fail to put across their agenda. For this reason they pillage the hegemonic discourse they seek to dismantle, and in doing so they usurp the weapons of their enemy. Hence it is one of the functions of an attitudinal stance, for which æsthetics provides the parameters, to point up what the respective oppositional discourses lack, thus alerting them to the fact that pure imitation or, worse still, repetition of what they are opposed to, should be replaced by an adequate form of rhetoric, for which again æsthetics might furnish the tools. However, if one argues along these lines, the irritation created is tremendous. And yet there is no effective substitute for the strategies of rationality, which is the main target of opposition. Aesthetics, therefore, one might argue, has a twofold function *vis à vis* the highly politicized oppositional discourses: on the one hand, it provides the basis for attitudinal stances that allow the thrust of these discourses to be assessed; and on the other, it may point out means of making them more effective.

Furthermore, the politicizing of the humanities results in reification of the stances advocated by group interests, whereas the humanities have always been engaged in a continuous process of self-definition. Therefore, these reified stances closely resemble the very definition of the past which the oppositional discourses set out to attack.

SECOND PART

March 27, 1994

SHAN TE-HSING: You are always interested in theory and its application to concrete texts. Can you elaborate on the applicability of your theory presented in your lectures here?

WOLFGANG ISER: My basic idea was to take a critical look at the presuppositions advanced in any act of interpretation. Even if we consider our presuppositions heuristic by nature, we are nevertheless inclined to say that the text means something specific, or is indicative of, let's say, a social situation or what have you. In other words, whenever we start out from presuppositions, we make the text in one way or another subservient to what the presupposition entails. For this reason we have to scrutinize interpretation in order to find out what actually happens when we are engaged in it.

The three lectures were concerned with different paradigms. The first addressed the question of how to understand the basic operation of interpretation through which a text is translated into a different register. Such a translation implies a circular movement between the text and the presuppositions brought to bear on it in the attempt to find out what it is supposed to mean.

My second lecture focused on interpretation of something non-textual. I chose culture as a paradigm. In this case you have to make an input from your own position, trying to carry it across to the culture concerned, from which you will get a response that may not tally with your original input, which therefore has to be corrected. Instead of a circular movement, you are engaged in a recursive one.

My third lecture dealt with a form of interpretation intended to translate something immeasurable, such as God, into cognition. The immeasurable defies any presupposition that one may be inclined to impose on it. Rather, it is in the nature of a potential, and if one wants to approximate it, one has to translate it into infinitesimal variables, none of which is individually able ever to represent this potential. Instead, the latter has to be unfolded into a sequence of graduated profiles, which continually shade into one another and thus draw it out into the open. For such a procedure the differential offers itself as a mode of cognitive translation.

In each of the three paradigms outlined, a circular, recursive, and differentiating operation effects the translation of something given into a different register that is at the heart of interpretation. – Circularity, recursion, and the differential are more often than not inscribed into one another in the various acts of interpretation. Their respective dominance or subservience depends upon whether it is a text, a culture, or an immeasurable that is to be interpreted. Interpreting a text implies a negotiation of positions; interpreting a culture, which is open-ended, implies moving from a stance to open-endedness in order to handle what is beyond immediate reach; interpreting something immeasurable implies carrying a potential across into a sequence of infinitesimally varying shapes that allow it to be grasped in terms of cognition.

In all acts of interpretation, the space between the subject matter and what it is transposed into can never be totally colonized. Of course, we start out from certain pre-suppositions, but then the presuppositions themselves should come under scrutiny. Such monitoring will result in a fine-tuning of our acts of interpretation, and so basic is interpretation to our profession that self-monitoring has now become essential.

SHAN TE-HSING: Since you have been here for a week and have given three lectures and one talk to a local audience, how would you interpret your interaction with this local audience in terms of your idea of cross-cultural relationship or 'recursive looping'? Can you take your visit as a concrete example?

WOLFGANG ISER: Initially I thought that, whatever my input, I would provoke a feedback of something that was not in my orbit prior to such an encounter. For this reason, the outcome of the interaction was important for me insofar as I became aware of limitations contained in the concepts I had put forward. Not that I had claimed universal validity for them, but I had considered them as tenable starting-points, and yet I learnt that they were conditioned by an inherent Western bias. Even if an audience is prepared to relate to Western views, one nevertheless gets a feedback that illuminates the restricted parameters of one's own ideas regarding the foreign culture. Thus all my inputs, which were just informed guesses, came back as corrected outputs. And when the recursive looping got under way, I began a fine-tuning process by feeding the corrections into my subsequent inputs. I took this to be a clear example of cross-cultural interchange insofar as there is no over-arching third dimension to govern the negotiation of what is different. Consequently, a cross-cultural interrelationship can only proceed by continually making the alien loop into the familiar in order to prevent an unreflected superimposition of one's own concepts on what is foreign.

SHAN TE-HSING: In addition to this intellectual exchange between you and the local audience, how would you interpret your personal experience of your encounter with our culture, for instance your visit to the National Palace Museum as a concrete personal example? How would you interpret it in terms of recursive looping?

WOLFGANG ISER: This is very hard to answer it in one sentence. Western tradition, in contradistinction to Chinese culture, tends to be individualistic. This may, among other things, account for the predominant commitment to politics as a means of getting things done, or asserting one's interests. Simultaneously, the West entertains an entrenched belief in rationality as an overriding guideline for achieving order and stability. I am only touching upon these features more or less *ad hoc* in order to point out a difference from what I have experienced here, in particular at the Museum, which exhibits all the treasures brought to Taipei from the mainland. The Museum does not seem merely to display the great past of China; instead, as a treasure house it reinforces the self-understanding of the culture. If one were to express it in a pedestrian banking term, one might be inclined to say the treasures are the collateral for the culture. Hence the bafflement of a Westerner faced with a culture like that of the Chinese, which is a tremendously neat and intricate symbol system for organizing life. Encountering such an elaborately mapped-out symbol system of an ancient culture which extends into the present was a striking experience for me. It gave me second thoughts as to the stability that Western rationality claims to achieve, not least as you can employ rationality for diverse and often contradictory purposes, which a rigid symbol system does not allow to any great degree.

SHAN TE-HSING: Can you say something more specific about your interaction with the local audience by taking your lecture series as an example?

WOLFGANG ISER   STEPPING FORWARD

WOLFGANG ISER: When I was pondering over my basic ideas for the lectures, it was hard for me to picture the kind of audience I was supposed to address. The questions raised in the discussions gave me food for thought insofar as I had not anticipated them and was frequently unable to fathom the nature of the experience that conditioned them. This was obvious in the responses to my outline of how the Judaic-Christian God can be translated into cognitive terms, as there is hardly anything comparable in Chinese culture; or when I was asked to assess the interlinear versions with which Chinese writers intersperse their texts in order to prescribe their meaning. Thus I learned a great deal about how to shape my thoughts in order to put across what I intended to say.

Almost every evening, when returning to the hotel, I put on tape how my ideas would have to be rearranged in order to remain convincing. It was immensely stimulating and beneficial to have an audience whose basic cultural disposition was so alien to what I was trying to describe. The feedback loop certainly generated an intensified self-monitoring of my own thinking, not least as I began to question myself regarding subject matters which had previously not dawned on me. My experience of an unexpected attitude being looped into my own ideas has brought me a long way forward in addressing the question of why human beings are constantly engaged in interpretation. I am very grateful for the opportunity to present my work-in-progress here in Taipei, and given the kind of feedback I have received, I am sure I shall be able to write a better book.

The interview was conducted in English, and subsequently published in Chinese in: *English and American Literature*, 2 (1995), pp. 197-211.

J.R.R. Tolkien
The Books, The Films, The Whole Cultural Phenomenon

by Jeremy Mark Robinson

A new critical study of J.R.R. Tolkien, creator of Middle-earth and author of *The Lord of the Rings, The Hobbit* and *The Silmarillion*, among other books.
This new critical study explores Tolkien's major writings (*The Lord of the Rings, The Hobbit, Beowulf: The Monster and the Critics, The Letters, The Silmarillion* and *The History of Middle-earth* volumes); Tolkien and fairy tales; the mythological, political and religious aspects of Tolkien's Middle-earth; the critics' response to Tolkien's fiction over the decades; the Tolkien industry (merchandizing, toys, role-playing games, posters, Tolkien societies, conferences and the like); Tolkien in visual and fantasy art; the cultural aspects of The Lord of the Rings (from the 1950s to the present); Tolkien's fiction's relationship with other fantasy fiction, such as C.S. Lewis and *Harry Potter*; and the TV, radio and film versions of Tolkien's books, including the 2001-03 Hollywood interpretations of *The Lord of the Rings*.
This new book draws on contemporary cultural theory and analysis and offers a sympathetic and illuminating (and sceptical) account of the Tolkien phenomenon. This book is designed to appeal to the general reader (and viewer) of Tolkien: it is written in a clear, jargon-free and easily-accessible style.

754pp   ISBN 1-86171-057-7   £25.00 / $37.50

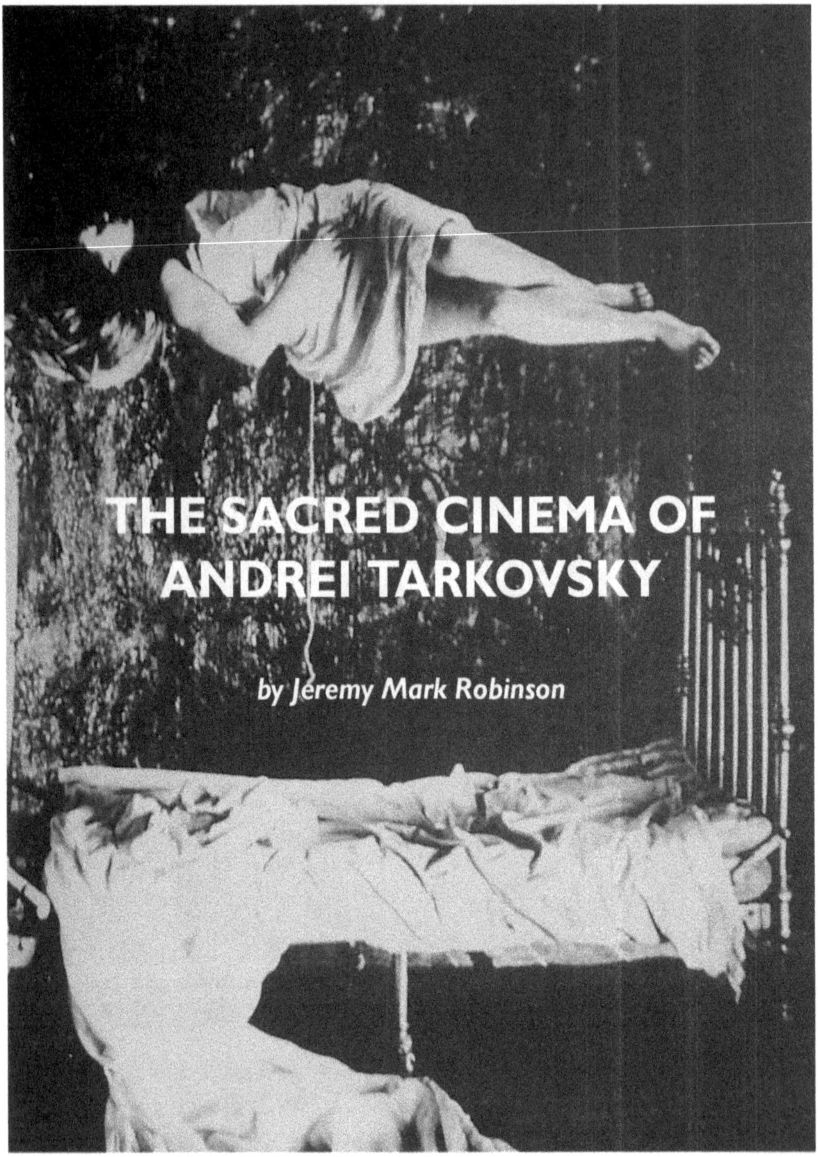

THE SACRED CINEMA OF ANDREI TARKOVSKY

by Jeremy Mark Robinson

A new study of the Russian filmmaker Andrei Tarkovsky (1932-1986), director of seven feature films, including *Andrei Roublyov, Mirror, Solaris, Stalker* and *The Sacrifice*.
This is one of the most comprehensive and detailed studies of Tarkovsky's cinema available. Every film is explored in depth, with scene-by-scene analyses. All aspects of Tarkovsky's output are critiqued, including editing, camera, staging, script, budget, collaborations, production, sound, music, performance and spirituality. Tarkovsky is placed with a European New Wave tradition of filmmaking, alongside directors like Ingmar Bergman, Carl Theodor Dreyer, Pier Paolo Pasolini and Robert Bresson.
An essential addition to film studies.

Illustrations: 150 b/w, 4 colour. 682 pages. First edition. Hardback.

Publisher: Crescent Moon Publishing. Distributor: Gardners Books.

ISBN 1-86171-096-8 (9781861710963) £60.00 / $105.00

The Best of Peter Redgrove's Poetry
The Book of Wonders

by Peter Redgrove, edited and introduced by Jeremy Robinson

Poems of wet shirts and 'wonder-awakening dresses'; honey, wasps and bees; orchards and apples; rivers, seas and tides; storms, rain, weather and clouds; waterworks; labyrinths; amazing perfumes; the Cornish landscape (Penzance, Perranporth, Falmouth, Boscastle, the Lizard and Scilly Isles); the sixth sense and 'extra-sensuous perception'; witchcraft; alchemical vessels and laboratories; yoga; menstruation; mines, minerals and stones; sand dunes; mud-baths; mythology; dreaming; vulvas; and lots of sex magic. This book gathers together poetry (and prose) from every stage of Redgrove's career, and every book. It includes pieces that have only appeared in small presses and magazines, and in uncollected form.

'Peter Redgrove is really an extraordinary poet' (George Szirtes, *Quarto* magazine)
'Peter Redgrove is one of the few significant poets now writing... His 'means' are indeed brilliant and delightful. Technically he is a poet essentially of brilliant and unexpected images...he never disappoints' (Kathleen Raine, *Temenos* magazine).

240pp   ISBN 1-86171-063-1   2nd edition   £19.99 / $29.50

Sex–Magic–Poetry–Cornwall
A Flood of Poems

by Peter Redgrove. Edited with an essay by Jeremy Robinson

A marvellous collection of poems by one of Britain's best but underrated poets, Peter Redgrove. This book brings together some of Redgrove's wildest and most passionate works, creating a 'flood' of poetry. Philip Hobsbaum called Redgrove 'the great poet of our time', while Angela Carter said: 'Redgrove's language can light up a page.' Redgrove ranks alongside Ted Hughes and Sylvia Plath. He is in every way a 'major poet'. Robinson's essay analyzes all of Redgrove's poetic work, including his use of sex magic, natural science, menstruation, psychology, myth, alchemy and feminism.
A new edition, including a new introduction, new preface and new bibliography.

'Robinson's enthusiasm is winning, and his perceptive readings are supported by a very useful bibliography' (*Acumen* magazine)
'*Sex-Magic-Poetry-Cornwall* is a very rich essay... It is like a brightly-lighted box. (Peter Redgrove)
'This is an excellent selection of poetry and an extensive essay on the themes and theories of this unusual poet by Jeremy Robinson' (*Chapman* magazine)

220pp   New, 3rd edition   ISBN 1-86171-070-4   £14.99 / $23.50

THE ART OF ANDY GOLDSWORTHY

COMPLETE WORKS: SPECIAL EDITION
(PAPERBACK and HARDBACK)

by William Malpas

A new, special edition of the study of the contemporary British sculptor, Andy Goldsworthy, including a new introduction, new bibliography and many new illustrations.

This is the most comprehensive, up-to-date, well-researched and in-depth account of Goldsworthy's art available anywhere.

Andy Goldsworthy makes land art. His sculpture is a sensitive, intuitive response to nature, light, time, growth, the seasons and the earth. Goldsworthy's environmental art is becoming ever more popular: 1993's art book *Stone* was a bestseller; the press raved about Goldsworthy taking over a number of London West End art galleries in 1994; during 1995 Goldsworthy designed a set of Royal Mail stamps and had a show at the British Museum. Malpas surveys all of Goldsworthy's art, and analyzes his relation with other land artists such as Robert Smithson, Walter de Maria, Richard Long and David Nash, and his place in the contemporary British art scene.

The Art of Andy Goldsworthy discusses all of Goldsworthy's important and recent exhibitions and books, including the *Sheepfolds* project; the TV documentaries; *Wood* (1996); the New York Holocaust memorial (2003); and Goldsworthy's collaboration on a dance performance.

Illustrations: 70 b/w, 1 colour. 330 pages. New, special, 2nd edition.
Publisher: Crescent Moon Publishing. Distributor: Gardners Books.

ISBN 1-86171-059-3 (9781861710598) (Paperback) £25.00 / $44.00

ISBN 1-86171-080-1 (9781861710802) (Hardback) £60.00 / $105.00

CRESCENT MOON PUBLISHING

ARTS, PAINTING, SCULPTURE

The Art of Andy Goldsworthy: Complete Works(Pbk)
The Art of Andy Goldsworthy: Complete Works (Hbk)
Andy Goldsworthy in Close-Up (Pbk)
Andy Goldsworthy in Close-Up (Hbk)
Land Art: A Complete Guide
Richard Long: The Art of Walking
The Art of Richard Long: Complete Works (Pbk)
The Art of Richard Long: Complete Works (Hbk)
Richard Long in Close-Up
Land Art In the UK
Land Art in Close-Up
Installation Art in Close-Up
Minimal Art and Artists In the 1960s and After
Colourfield Painting
Land Art DVD, TV documentary
Andy Goldsworthy DVD, TV documentary
The Erotic Object: Sexuality in Sculpture From Prehistory to the Present Day
Sex in Art: Pornography and Pleasure in Painting and Sculpture
Postwar Art
Sacred Gardens: The Garden in Myth, Religion and Art
Glorification: Religious Abstraction in Renaissance and 20th Century Art
Early Netherlandish Painting
Leonardo da Vinci
Piero della Francesca
Giovanni Bellini
Fra Angelico: Art and Religion in the Renaissance
Mark Rothko: The Art of Transcendence
Frank Stella: American Abstract Artist
Jasper Johns: Painting By Numbers
Brice Marden
Alison Wilding: The Embrace of Sculpture
Vincent van Gogh: Visionary Landscapes
Eric Gill: Nuptials of God
Constantin Brancusi: Sculpting the Essence of Things
Max Beckmann
Egon Schiele: Sex and Death In Purple Stockings
Delizioso Fotografico Fervore: Works In Process 1
Sacro Cuore: Works In Process 2
The Light Eternal: J.M.W. Turner
The Madonna Glorified: Karen Arthurs

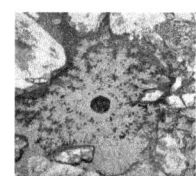

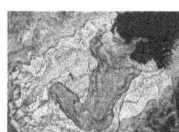

LITERATURE

J.R.R. Tolkien: The Books, The Films, The Whole Cultural Phenomenon
Harry Potter
Sexing Hardy: Thomas Hardy and Feminism
Thomas Hardy's *Tess of the d'Urbervilles*
Thomas Hardy's *Jude the Obscure*
Thomas Hardy: The Tragic Novels
Love and Tragedy: Thomas Hardy
The Poetry of Landscape in Hardy
Wessex Revisited: Thomas Hardy and John Cowper Powys
Wolfgang Iser: Essays
Petrarch, Dante and the Troubadours
Maurice Sendak and the Art of Children's Book Illustration
Andrea Dworkin
Cixous, Irigaray, Kristeva: The *Jouissance* of French Feminism
Julia Kristeva: Art, Love, Melancholy, Philosophy, Semiotics and Psychoanalysis
Hélène Cixous I Love You: The *Jouissance* of Writing
Luce Irigaray: Lips, Kissing, and the Politics of Sexual Difference
Peter Redgrove: Here Comes the Flood
Peter Redgrove: Sex-Magic-Poetry-Cornwall
Lawrence Durrell: Between Love and Death, East and West
Love, Culture & Poetry: Lawrence Durrell
Cavafy: Anatomy of a Soul
German Romantic Poetry: Goethe, Novalis, Heine, Hölderlin, Schlegel, Schiller
Feminism and Shakespeare
Shakespeare: Selected Sonnets
Shakespeare: Love, Poetry & Magic
The Passion of D.H. Lawrence
D.H. Lawrence: Symbolic Landscapes
D.H. Lawrence: Infinite Sensual Violence
Rimbaud: Arthur Rimbaud and the Magic of Poetry
The Ecstasies of John Cowper Powys
Sensualism and Mythology: The Wessex Novels of John Cowper Powys
Amorous Life: John Cowper Powys and the Manifestation of Affectivity (H.W. Fawkner)
Postmodern Powys: New Essays on John Cowper Powys (Joe Boulter)
Rethinking Powys: Critical Essays on John Cowper Powys
Paul Bowles & Bernardo Bertolucci
Rainer Maria Rilke
In the Dim Void: Samuel Beckett
Samuel Beckett Goes into the Silence
André Gide: Fiction and Fervour
Jackie Collins and the Blockbuster Novel
Blinded By Her Light: The Love-Poetry of Robert Graves
The Passion of Colours: Travels In Mediterranean Lands
Poetic Forms
The Dolphin-Boy

POETRY

The Best of Peter Redgrove's Poetry
Peter Redgrove: Here Comes The Flood
Peter Redgrove: Sex-Magic-Poetry-Cornwall
Ursula Le Guin: Walking In Cornwall
Dante: Selections From the Vita Nuova
Petrarch, Dante and the Troubadours
William Shakespeare: Selected Sonnets
Blinded By Her Light: The Love-Poetry of Robert Graves
Emily Dickinson: Selected Poems
Emily Brontë: Poems
Thomas Hardy: Selected Poems
Percy Bysshe Shelley: Poems
John Keats: Selected Poems
D.H. Lawrence: Selected Poems
Edmund Spenser: Poems
John Donne: Poems
Henry Vaughan: Poems
Sir Thomas Wyatt: Poems
Robert Herrick: Selected Poems
Rilke: Space, Essence and Angels in the Poetry of Rainer Maria Rilke
Rainer Maria Rilke: Selected Poems
Friedrich Hölderlin: Selected Poems
Arseny Tarkovsky: Selected Poems
Arthur Rimbaud: Selected Poems
Arthur Rimbaud: A Season in Hell
Arthur Rimbaud and the Magic of Poetry
D.J. Enright: By-Blows
Jeremy Reed: Brigitte's Blue Heart
Jeremy Reed: Claudia Schiffer's Red Shoes
Gorgeous Little Orpheus
Radiance: New Poems
Crescent Moon Book of Nature Poetry
Crescent Moon Book of Love Poetry
Crescent Moon Book of Mystical Poetry
Crescent Moon Book of Elizabethan Love Poetry
Crescent Moon Book of Metaphysical Poetry
Crescent Moon Book of Romantic Poetry
Pagan America: New American Poetry

MEDIA, CINEMA, FEMINISM and CULTURAL STUDIES

J.R.R. Tolkien: The Books, The Films, The Whole Cultural Phenomenon
Harry Potter
Cixous, Irigaray, Kristeva: The *Jouissance* of French Feminism
Julia Kristeva: Art, Love, Melancholy, Philosophy, Semiotics and Psychoanalysis
Luce Irigaray: Lips, Kissing, and the Politics of Sexual Difference
Hélene Cixous I Love You: The *Jouissance* of Writing
Andrea Dworkin
'Cosmo Woman': The World of Women's Magazines
Women in Pop Music
Discovering the Goddess (Geoffrey Ashe)
The Poetry of Cinema
The Sacred Cinema of Andrei Tarkovsky (Pbk and Hbk)
Paul Bowles & Bernardo Bertolucci
Media Hell: Radio, TV and the Press
An Open Letter to the BBC
Detonation Britain: Nuclear War in the UK
Feminism and Shakespeare
Wild Zones: Pornography, Art and Feminism
Sex in Art: Pornography and Pleasure in Painting and Sculpture
Sexing Hardy: Thomas Hardy and Feminism

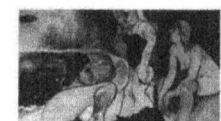
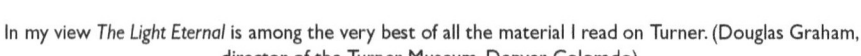

In my view *The Light Eternal* is among the very best of all the material I read on Turner. (Douglas Graham, director of the Turner Museum, Denver, Colorado)

The Light Eternal is a model monograph, an exemplary job. The subject matter of the book is beautifully organised and dead on beam. (Lawrence Durrell)

It is amazing for me to see my work treated with such passion and respect. (Andrea Dworkin)

Sex-Magic-Poetry-Cornwall is a very rich essay... It is like a brightly-lighted box. (Peter Redgrove)

CRESCENT MOON PUBLISHING
P.O. Box 393, Maidstone, Kent, ME14 5XU, United Kingdom.
01622-729593 (UK) 01144-1622-729593 (US) 0044-1622-729593 (other territories)
cresmopub@yahoo.co.uk   www.crescentmoon.org.uk

www.ingramcontent.com/pod-product-compliance
Lightning Source LLC
Chambersburg PA
CBHW070324100426
42743CB00011B/2544